War for the West
1790–1813

War for the West
1790-1813

HARRISON BIRD

New York OXFORD UNIVERSITY PRESS 1971

In grateful and admiring memory of

E.M.

Acknowledgments

Not until an author has completed the work on his book does he realize the help that he has received, and can take the opportunity to acknowledge it.

Help comes in many forms, not least in the patience of those around him in his own home, where he is apt to be working. I acknowledge and appreciate the forbearance, as well as the actual aid, of my wife, Harriette Jansen Bird, through this and all the other books before it.

Directly pertinent assistance comes so willingly from friends when it is asked. Mrs. John Nicholas Brown not only made available for this book, as for previous ones, illustrations from her superb collection, but also, from her deep knowledge of graphic art, she was kind enough to suggest those pictures which would be most interesting and appropriate. John Cuneo lent me books from his excellent and specialized library, and he allowed me to keep them for long periods of time! In Dr. George F. Stanley, I was fortunate in having a friend on the

Canadian side of the War, who willingly supplied facts and clarification.

Individuals in groups and institutions were helpful because it is their way. I am always grateful to the Members of the Company of Military Historians for their personal encouragement, and for the research work they do and place on record. The help given by the staffs of libraries, particularly those at my home library, the Crandall Library at Glens Falls, New York, and those in the American History Room at the New York Public Library, makes an author's task infinitely easier and more pleasant.

In the writing of this book there were those who provided helpful assistance, and I acknowledge with thanks that of W. Hoffman Benjamin, Frances Foster, S. Ely Goldsmith, Eugene P. Lynch, and Edward Mann.

Finally, I wish to thank Betsy Delay, who carefully, cheerfully, and promptly typed the manuscript.

Contents

Maps

War for the West
1790–1813

I

The Chief and the Governor

Tecumseh arrived at the council at Vincennes with four hundred warriors at his back. All were armed. All were young. All were arrogant. The people of the capital of Indiana Territory were alarmed. They had expected the Shawnee chief to bring a fitting escort—perhaps thirty warriors—from his town on the upper Wabash. Faced with a belligerent horde camped in the woods, the townspeople barricaded their doors while the militia increased their patrols. Even the Methodist minister kept himself near to a loaded musket. In his mansion, *Grouseland,* William Henry Harrison, Governor of Indiana Territory, calmly prepared to meet his Indian guest the following day, Tuesday, 13 August 1811. He planned to meet with Tecumseh and his chiefs under a portico of the house.

On the morning of the appointed day, Tecumseh, with thrity councilors and his escort, drew near to where Harrison waited with an honor guard of twelve uniformed militiamen. Tecumseh's four hundred warriors waited within call in the woods near by. All the citizens of Vincennes had gathered in the cleared meadow in front of *Grouseland,* but the meeting did not take place as staged. Tecumseh refused to enter under the white man's roof. The sun was the Indians' father, he said, and the Indians made council under the sky in the presence of their father.

With the patience of a statesman, William Henry Harrison had two chairs placed under a tree in the grove where Tecumseh waited. From there he could see his big house and from the grove the Indians in the wood could hear their leader's words. With his honor guard ranged behind him, William Henry Harrison sat down in one of the chairs, placed his scabbard and sword comfortably beside him, and prepared to listen.

Tecumseh spoke. He spoke in his own tongue, and the inhabitants of Vincennes, who knew the Shawnee as a great orator, heard the cooing of a dove at morning, the boastful drumming of a grouse on a log, the screech of an eagle diving to protect her nest. The Indians, listening to the words and images of speech, grunted their approval of the insolent taunts their leader flung at the feet of the white chief. Harrison listened to the translator tell of the Shawnee's claim to leadership of all the Indian nations living between the Ohio and the Great Lakes. He heard the repudiation of his purchase of land from the several nations living there, and he heard Tecumseh threaten the lives of the "village chiefs" who had sold what was not theirs to sell. Harrison listened to the chief's demand that the Americans return the land to Tecumseh's confederation. In that demand there was the threat of unbridled war.

Governor Harrison listened attentively to the translation and, through the interpreter, invited the chief to sit in the chair beside him. For the second time that day, the Shawnee rebuffed the governor. He sat down on the ground, Indian fashion, remarking loudly that as the sun was his father so the earth was his mother. The warriors heard with approval and marked the gesture as one that laid claim to the land.

Patiently, William Henry Harrison rose from his seat. He spoke in English, knowing that Tecumseh understood the language well. He made no mention of the treaty he had made with the chiefs of the Miami, Potawatomi, Delaware, Wea, and Eel River Indians, by which, in fair trade, he had purchased three million acres of tribal land for the United States. With scorn in his voice, Harrison turned his words to an attack on Tecumseh's claim of Indian unity under confederation. How could Tecumseh count the nations a single people when the Great Spirit had given them six different tongues? As the interpreter translated into the language that Tecumseh had used, Harrison eased the sword hanging at his left side. When the governor spoke again, he challenged Tecumseh's claim to leadership and scorned his people. How could he, a Shawnee, presume to dispose of land owned by the Miami nation and already sold by the chiefs of that nation? Were not the Shawnee only guests of the Miami, since the Creek had driven the Shawnee from their homeland in Georgia?

Before a translation could be made for the benefit of the listening Indians, Tecumseh was on his feet, giving the lie straight to the governor's face. Harrison took a half pace forward and drew his sword. Tecumseh's hand fell as easily to the handle of his tomahawk. The twelve militia guards clicked back the hammers of their muskets, passed the half, to the full cock. The four hundred followers of Tecumseh edged forward, readying their weapons. The Methodist minister ran for the front door of *Grouseland*, where, just inside, stood a loaded musket.

For the eternity of a long moment nothing happened. Then the anger subsided and the two tall men stood facing each other, each back on his own side of the thin line of reason. But the fruitless council was over.

Harrison and Tecumseh met once again before the Indian took his people back up the Wabash River to their town on Tippecanoe Creek. The governor sought out the chief in his camp, and the white man and the red man talked alone, sitting easily together on a log. Both were civilized men.

II

Tecumseh

For almost twenty years Tecumseh and William Henry Harrison, in the same space and at the same time, had devoted their energy to similar ambitions and conflicting purposes. At the council at Vincennes in August 1811, the Indian was completely dedicated and committed to his concept of uniting the council fires of all the Indian nations into a federation, to hold their land in common for their race. The white man, sitting in his chair under the council tree, was determined to unite his Territory of Indiana with the federation of states, which so recently had been proclaimed east of the Allegheny Mountains, and which already had spread westward to include Kentucky and Ohio.

Though each man pursued his separate destiny in the rich lands north and west of the Ohio River, neither the chief nor the governor was truly a native of "The Northwest," as the region was then called.

Tecumseh had been born there in the Indian town of Piqua, on the bluffs above the Mad River. He was the son of

7

Pukeshinwa, a displaced Shawnee war chief who had been
born in Spanish Florida, far from the lost homeland of the
Shawnee nation in colonial Georgia. From his base in Florida,
Pukeshinwa had fought the British and their allies, the Creek,
who had taken the Shawnee homeland for their own. Pukeshinwa was in Alabama, fighting the old enemy from that
quarter, when he took a wife. Then, with his band of warriors,
he emigrated north to the land of the hospitable Miami, where
he was made welcome by the other migrant Shawnee who had
settled in the town of Piqua. While his wife bore him children
in "the town raised from ashes," which is the meaning of
"Piqua," Pukeshinwa carried on the Shawnee war against the
British colonists, pressing westward over the Alleghenies into
the Indian lands.

The boy Tecumseh grew up in the sprawling town of bark
cabins and wigwams on the bluffs. He played with his brothers
and the other boys on the banks of the river and in the
cornfields, whose tall stalks made fine spears for the game of
war. Tecumseh's father was often away, making real war in
the "dark and bloody ground" of Kentucky, across the Ohio
River. Though Pukeshinwa and the other bands ambushed,
killed, plundered, and burned the settlers, who now called
themselves Americans, the white men could not be turned
back.

Tecumseh was still a little boy when the family of Logan,
the "friend of the white man," was butchered in a white man's
town. That mass murder of Indians was talked over wherever
little Indian boys listened, and hearing, they learned who their
enemy was. The white man's treacherous ways were under-
lined when, in 1777, the revered Shawnee chief, Cornstalk,

and his son, were killed out of hand while on a friendly visit to a white man's fort. When Pukeshinwa was shot dead by marauding white men, Tecumseh was ready and old enough to begin his training as a warrior. Blackfish, the war chief of the Chillicothe-on-the-Little-Miami Shawnee, and the captor and foster father of Daniel Boone, undertook the education in war and leadership of his friend's young son. Before Tecumseh's education in weaponry, woodcraft, endurance, command, and oratory could be completed, Blackfish was killed, successfully defending Chillicothe against raiders from Kentucky.

The bloody years of Tecumseh's boyhood, from seven to fifteen, were the calendar years of the American War of Independence (1775–83). That war, fought out along the Atlantic seaboard, spilled over into the land west of the mountains and for its duration absorbed the continuing war of the Shawnee. It also brought to the Indians of the Northwest an active ally in the British from Canada.

Captain Henry Bird, who came to Piqua in the spring of 1780, was a regular officer on the British establishment. He came to the Shawnee town with a big war party of Wyandot and Mingo. Bird's purpose, and the purpose of the special cadre of woods-trained British regulars who came with him, was to rouse the warriors of Piqua to go on a rampage through the American settlements along the Licking River in Kentucky. The British soldiers brought with them two great cannon, the first Tecumseh had seen, to batter down the log stockades of the American forts. Bird and the other British officers seconded to the Indian service were instruments of British policy, dictated by London and administered from Canada. By aid in materiel, instruction, and leadership, the

British hoped to preserve the Indian nations as a buffer against the western surge of the Americans and as a friendly bridge to British ambition still further west. In Piqua in 1780, Captain Bird's appeal, and the appeal of the cannon, brought enthusiastic support from the Shawnee of Piqua and of Chillicothe.

Tecumseh was twelve years old the day that the British and their cannon, with a thousand Indians, set out for the Licking River. There was great feasting in Piqua when the party returned. The fighting men told of the wonder-filled power of the cannon, how it roared like thunder, and how it had snapped like twigs the picket logs at Ruddle's and Martin's forts. They told how the American commanders had surrendered to the voice of the gun, and they boasted of the killing they had done of the prisoners, men, women, and children, that they found cowering within the broken, open walls. The return warriors showed proudly some two hundred drying hanks of scalp hair, and paraded to scorn almost one hundred prisoners.

Later that summer of 1780, George Rogers Clark came to Piqua to avenge the business on the Licking River. Clark was an American, tall, red-headed, and as respected as he was dreaded by the Indians in all the Northwest. He was a Virginian who raised and led Kentuckians in their war against the British and their Indian allies in the trans-mountain lands. As a master of forest warfare, Colonel Clark was as well known along the Mississippi as he was to the Shawnee of Piqua on the Mad River.

Tecumseh, roused by the first alarm, heard the shouted orders and then the vague, detached flurry of still meaningless musketfire. He heard the dull thump of a cannon, firing from afar. He ran to see a collapsed wigwam, struck by the first iron cannon ball. The musketfire was drawing closer as the Indians fell back, and growing louder and spreading around the town as the enemy attempted to envelop Piqua. People whom Tecumseh knew were running now, away from the sound, toward the cornfields and the forest beyond. Tecumseh ran as only a scared boy can run. His flying feet pounded the long lane between the rustling stalks of tasseled corn. In the deep woods there was quiet, broken only by the pounding of a frightened heart in the chest of the small boy.

Colonel Clark, the scourge of the Indians, the instrument of the Kentuckians' revenge, stood among the flaming lodges of Piqua. At his direction, the Kentucky men galloped through the ripened corn, fire brands in their hands. By then, the frightened Indian boy was well into the woods and running hard. He would have a hungry winter that year.

Piqua was built again in a new place on the Miami River, and to it came the Shawnee of Chillicothe, who also had been left homeless by George Rogers Clark. There Tecumseh continued his schooling for war. He attached himself to his elder brother, Cheeseekau, and at fourteen he was old enough and strong enough to go, but not yet to fight, on an Anglo-Indian raid to the Licking River. Soon after his return from Kentucky, Tecumseh was caught in an ambush and had to fight or run. When he saw his brother fall wounded, Tecumseh ran. He never again ran from an enemy. Sometime during that evening in the Indian camp, as Cheeseekau salved his wound, Tecumseh conquered all fear for himself. Tecumseh means "Shooting Star" in the Shawnee tongue: that night, Tecumseh's star began its rise into the Indian sky.

In another year Tecumseh was fifteen and an accepted warrior among the Shawnee. The Anglo-American war in the east was all but over. The restlessness of peace seized the citizens of the new United States of America. The migration into the new lands to the west increased to a flood. The tempo of the Indians' war against the newcomers increased. A favorite route of homesteading Americans was by flatboat down the course of the Ohio River. Whole families took to the waters of the beautiful river, a few stock cattle tethered in the bow of the boat. Household goods, tools, and precious bags of seed were piled amidship, a child or two on top. In the stern, the man and woman tugged and pulled at the sweep as they searched for the current which would take them all to the hoped-for land downriver.

The banks of the Ohio became a place of ambush for the Indians of the Northwest, and the innocent flatboaters were easy prey. Tecumseh's band of Indians was often there and the young warrior learned where the river current brought the cumbersome boats closest to shore, and where the families landed to camp and graze their cattle.

It was here along the river that Tecumseh, while still in his mid-teens, stood against the Indian custom of torturing useless prisoners. A hapless American had been caught, and as none of his captors wanted him for adoption nor was he worth ransoming, his captors, as a diversion, prepared to burn him at the stake. The young Tecumseh, one of the war party, refused to take part in the ceremony. Once it had begun, moreover, Tecumseh jumped to his feet and, using all the oratory he had learned from his father and from Blackfish, he persuaded his comrades to spare the wretched victim.

That Tecumseh was sensitive to cruelty did not cause him to be shunned by the other warriors. They recognized the powers of leadership, as well as the courage, cunning, and strength that showed early in the young warrior. He became a trusted scout for the war parties, watching the river for flatboats.

The Treaty of Paris, which ended the eight-year war between Britain and her colonies in North America, had its effect on the Indian war in Kentucky and the Northwest. By the terms of the treaty, Britain gave up all claims to the land below the Great Lakes and retired into Canada. The United States of America took title to the disputed land and administered it as a territory, with the intent of subdividing the vast region into states as the white population increased sufficiently to warrant self-government. The Indians who lived in the Northwest were not signatories to the treaty nor were they consulted by either party. The powerful Miami and other indigenous nations, with the Shawnee newcomers, continued the war for autonomy of their homeland. Released by the ending of hostilities on the eastern seaboard, and encouraged by their victory over Britain, the Americans were moving west in a surge of energy. Not only did they continue to enter into Kentucky from Virginia, but settlers from New England began to populate the eastern part of the Northwest, which they called Ohio. The Indians north of the Ohio River were now in direct confrontation with the Americans. In the first years following the peace treaty, the Indian cause prospered. The ambushes along the Ohio River and raids in the eastern region slowed down the Americans' surge into the Northwest. In this effort, the Indian nations were aided by the British in Canada. Far from abandoning their policy of forming an Indian buffer state, the British fostered it by sending military aid to the chiefs, along with political propagandists who encouraged friendship. By haggling over the terms of the treaty, Britain still occupied Detroit, the town and trading post they had already ceded. British soldiers even resurrected and garrisoned an old abandoned fort on the Maumee River in United States territory. The fort was a crossroad, convenient for the distribution to the Indians, especially to the Miami, of guns, lead, and powder.

Tecumseh had become a leader of Shawnee scouts in the years immediately following the end of the American War of Independence. He also became a wanderer. No longer was there a lodge in Piqua to which he could return. His mother had gone back to her own people in the south. Tecumseh was visiting her in Alabama when a final tragedy struck close to him. During a raid on a schoolhouse, his brother Cheeseekau was killed. The war party had driven the class into the log school and was battering on the barred door. Through a chink, the Indians could see the schoolmaster leading the children in a last hymn, and through the opening, wide enough to sight a musket, the schoolmaster was shot dead. The boys and girls fought for their lives. Before rescue came, the boy, Hugh Rogan, had shot and killed Cheeseekau. Tecumseh returned north to continue his war.

III

William Henry Harrison Goes West

At heart, George Washington was a western man. In his youth he had gone over the mountains as a spy and as a soldier on three campaigns that won the west for Britain and for her colonies, pressed onto the Atlantic coastal plain. The young Washington had built the first wagon road over the forbidding hills, and in all his deeds and actions in the beckoning land beyond the Alleghenies, he had made his reputation as a leader among men. He owned forty thousand potentially valuable acres in Kentucky when Destiny called him to lead the thirteen Atlantic colonies in the Revolution. His duty discharged, Washington, now a mature man, turned again to the west. His dream was a canal between the Potomac and the Ohio rivers, to bind by commercial communication the nation of the east and the nation of the west into one strong and great country. Washington took that dream with him into office as President of the newly constituted United States of America.

Less than two years after becoming President, in a simple, routine act of office George Washington assured the unity of the west and the east, and projected himself into the future as a western man. On 16 August 1791, President Washington commissioned William Henry Harrison an ensign in the First Regiment of Infantry. It was a small favor to do for a likely boy who was the son of an old and valued friend, so recently dead.

There was no patrimony for William Henry Harrison, the fifteenth child of his esteemed father. There are few tangible rewards for rebellion, revolution, and reconstruction, and Benjamin Harrison, first in the colony and then in the state of Virginia, had devoted his life to serving those ends. William Henry, his youngest son, was born on February 9, 1773, not long before the Revolution began, and he had suffered from his father's dedication to contrary principles. Before he was eight years old he was forced to flee the security of *Berkeley*, the quiet brick home of the Harrison family. The alarm was out that the traitor, General Arnold, was marauding toward Richmond with his Tory Rangers and Redcoats, and *Berkeley* lay on his line of march. Later young William Henry had been brought back to a ransacked house, wantonly pillaged. He had been shown the family's pride, portraits of earlier Harrisons of distinction, reduced to gray ashes on the hoof-trampled lawn.

William Henry Harrison studied and attended college during the lean years following the Revolution, so he was a well-formed young man of his times in the spring of 1791, when his father's death thrust him into the world. The loyalty of faithful friends in high places was an intangible legacy of the father to his children, and President Washington's friendship for his father opened for young Harrison a career of public service that began in the army. In 1775, Benjamin Harrison had ridden north to serve in the Second Continental Congress with his Tidewater neighbor, George Washington. The friendship had lasted, and the political obligation it imposed was easily met by the commission that Washington, as Commander in Chief, signed on 16 August 1791.

That the First Regiment of Infantry was operating in the west and that the new ensign would be serving there was fitting, both for Washington and for the son of Benjamin Harrison. As a political leader in Virginia during the Revolution, Benjamin Harrison had enabled George Rogers Clark to raise an army and carry out his campaigns in the west. The intent of the sometime governor of Virginia had been more than protect the settlers and settlements in the county of Kentucky. Clark's mission had been against the British as well as the Indians, and his goal had been the winning of the Northwest. As the harsh reality of George Rogers Clark's conquest had destroyed the home of a frightened little Indian boy, so, too, had little William Henry Harrison known the destruction in the wake of the maurauding Arnold. Now, in 1791, Benjamin Harrison's son, a young ensign, was going west to make secure the victory his father had helped to gain. Tecumseh, whose home Clark had destroyed, in 1791 was a bold young leader of Indian scouts, bound to thwart the conquest of the Northwest by the United States.

Washington and Harrison had long been aware of the problems involved in holding the distant western lands, problems not to be solved immediately by sending the son of one of them to fight Indians there. The first wave of settlers had gone to Kentucky just prior to the outbreak of the War of Independence. The migration had continued throughout the war that raged up and down the eastern seaboard. The aims and principles of the Revolution had scarcely affected the life of the trans-Allegheny settler, determined as he was to establish his family on his own holdings and to fight the Indians who disputed his right to the land. The Treaty of Paris, signed in a remote Europe by two distant governments, placed the western settler back under the now united colony-states, which earlier they had abandoned to seek their own individual independence in a far place. The original western homesteader was not imbued with a fierce loyalty to the United States, nor could the post-Revolutionary War immigrants be expected to be enthusiastic American citizens. Washington pointed this out in a letter to Benjamin Harrison, dated October 1784. In general, the new settlers in the west were malcontents from the east, those ever-hopeful failures from the old thirteen colonies, and European immigrants who passed quickly through the Atlantic ports, hurrying onward to the Land of Promise in the Northwest.

The tenuous nature of the settlers' loyalty to the United States was accentuated by their separation from their government. Few of the migrant families had forgotten their arduous journey over the dividing wall of the Allegheny Mountains. Separated thus by the immensity of their journey and the loom of those terrible mountains, the western citizens, as Washington pointed out to Benjamin Harrison, would look away from the east for trade, commerce, and friendship, and, ultimately, for alliance. Spain, at the mouth of the Mississippi highway, and England, on the Great Lakes–St. Lawrence waterway, were the adjacent neighbors of the western Americans. To forestall the seduction of the west by these two formidable powers, Washington proposed the Potomac–Ohio river canal. By building a good avenue of communication through those terrible mountains, and by developing a flow of imports and exports, Washington hoped to join the westerners with the easterners in friendly, beneficial interdependence. Benjamin Harrison agreed to co-operate in promoting the canal.

The canal project was dormant when George Washington took office as President, but he immediately set about promoting unification by other means. As Minister of State, Thomas Jefferson employed all the wiles of diplomacy in an effort to keep Spain and Britain out of the west. By promising and encouraging full statehood, the United States Government sought to strengthen the ties between east and west. In 1791, Kentucky County of Virginia was already approaching the population figure that was a prerequisite for statehood. The North Carolinians settling Tennessee were growing toward the same goal, and in the "Indian Lands" of the Northwest the boundaries of Ohio were taking shape. The government sent good men to the west to administer the laws, to treat with the Indians and to lead the settlers until local inhabitants could be trained to manage their own affairs. And Washington, the soldier, sent soldiers to fulfill a government's first obligation: the protection of its citizens and its territory.

But President Washington had few soldiers to send to quell the mounting fury of the continuing Indian raids that were generated in the interior of the Northwest Territory. Although the architects of confederation had given the President the title and duties of Commander in Chief, the Congress, like the Continental Congress before it, was reluctant to authorize the creation of an army to implement the title. The Continental Congress had expressed itself succinctly: "Standing armies in time of peace are inconsistent with the principles of republican government, dangerous to the liberties of a free people, and generally converted into destructive engines for establishing despotism." With these words in requiem, General Washington's Army of Continentals had been dismissed at the conclusion of the War of Independence without thanks and without full pay. By June of 1784, the United States army consisted of one captain and eighty men to janitor government stores at West Point on the Hudson River and at Pittsburgh where the west began with the Ohio.

The Founding Fathers, however, did recognize that local problems, calling for defensive and even punitive measures, would arise. As Minute Men had sprung to arms to guard the martial stores at Concord, so Congress would call on the state or states involved to quell disorders with their volunteer militia. The militant Indians of the west provided such a disorder, and the day after their denunciation of standing armies the Congress called upon four states, Connecticut, New York, New Jersey, and Pennsylvania, to provide a total of seven hundred men to keep the peace in the Ohio River valley. This force, which never achieved its full strength in the year for which it was called out, neither defended the settlers nor intimidated the Indians, nor did it impress the Spanish and British beyond the western borders. It could scarcely defend itself in its own passage between the stockade forts that it manned along the river. The conglomerate of state militiamen did, however, contain one soldier of ability. Josiah Harmar had been an officer of the Continentals from 1775 until they were disbanded. He was a lieutenant colonel of the Pennsylvania militia when that state answered the call of Congress for two hundred and sixty militiamen to go west. As Harmar commanded the Pennsylvanians, and as his was numerically the largest contingent, he was given command of the whole. Trained under Washington and experienced in the management of men, Colonel Harmar set out to make the divers elements of his force into a united army. He did it by bravado. He called himself "General," and the men under him he called "The First American Regiment." Under that banner, borne on the strong staff of its general, the United States army had its beginning.

Before the year's enlistment of the seven hundred was over, Congress recognized that too few soldiers had been called for too short a time. The term of enlistment was extended to three years and the enrollment increased until, at the end of the year, Congress had authorized two thousand forty soldiers for the army, though the congressmen preferred the classical title of "legionary corps." "General" Harmar's "First American Regiment" provided the shell in which the army grew. The creation of two companies of artillery gave credence to the pretense of the "general" who actually had the rank and pay of a lieutenant colonel.

Yet when the federal government came into being and George Washington again was Commander in Chief and a war department was set up, Harmar had less than six hundred men under arms. Nor was the great and honored Washington immediately able to establish an army such as he had once led. In March of 1791 the intensity of the Indian raids in the Northwest had so increased, and with them, the clamor for federal protection, that a 2nd Regiment of Infantry was authorized, as well as a staff under a major general to coordinate the expanded army.

Nineteen-year-old William Henry Harrison entered the army (referred to by a wary Congress as "the Service of the United States") under the expansion. In his bright new uniform of blue the boy rode west, a replacement officer for the old First American Regiment, now the 1st Regiment of Infantry.

IV

First Blood for the 1st

The 1st Regiment of U.S. Infantry was in need of replacements. The regiment had taken casualties in 1790, and as Ensign Harrison descended the mountain road into the Ohio River valley, the troops were out in force again on yet another raid in strength into the interior of the Northwest Territory. They could expect more casualties before they returned.

Arthur St. Clair, hapless general of the Revolution and now governor of the Northwest Territory, had made binding treaties with the Indian nations at a council held in the spring of 1789 at Fort Harmar, at the mouth of the Muskingum River. There the chiefs of six nations, Chippewa, Delaware, Ottawa, Potawatomi, Sac, and Wyandot, had confirmed the boundaries and agreed on compensations. The powerful Miami, however, had been pointedly absent from Fort Harmar and had expressed their opposition to this council by intensifying their raids on the flatboat traffic down the Ohio. The westward movement of immigration was cut off at Pittsburgh that summer of 1789, and from the intelligence that came into the governor's office, it appeared that the threat to the security of all the Northwest Territory would increase in 1790.

Major John Hamtramck of the 1st American Regiment commanded at Vincennes on the Wabash River. He was Canadian-born, and people of his town were of the old French-Canadian *voyageur* and trader stock who moved freely among the tribes to trade or to visit relatives or connections. Hamtramck used his Frenchmen as spies and messengers to the Miami and the Shawnee. They all brought back tales of British involvement and influence. The English at Detroit were encouraging the young men to raid the Americans. The British agent was making gifts of guns and powder and lead. Said the Indians: "The English commander is our father since he threw down our French father. We cannot go against his wishes."

Major Hamtramck had told all this to Governor St. Clair, who, in turn, sought guidance and help from his government in Philadelphia. Not wishing to become embroiled with England, or with the Spanish, who were encouraging Indian trouble in the south, the Congress chose to consider the Ohio raids as a local affair, wholly within the province of the governor of the Northwest Territory. Arthur St. Clair then turned to the western counties of Virginia and Pennsylvania for aid, and ordered Colonel Harmar to mount a punitive campaign against the main Miami towns. The time would be the summer of 1790. The rallying place would be Fort Washington, not yet called Cincinnati.

There was work to be done on the farm clearings scattered through the valley lands of Kentucky and Pennsylvania. When the call to muster came to the militiaman farmer, his hay was not yet ready for cutting, the rows and hillocks of corn needed tending, and the truck was struggling up with the weeds. There was much urgent work to be done on the farm and he did it, hastily, before taking the road to the river and the growing camp outside the weathered log walls of Fort Washington.

Scattered though they were among the distant outposts of the frontier, the available soldiers of the 1st Regiment came to the rendezvous, as did the militiamen. The officers commanding the blockhouses grumbled as they pared down their garrisons on orders of the "General." The lucky ones went to Fort Washington with their own contingents. Those left behind shut and barred the gates and waited for the Indians to come or for their troops to return.

General Harmar set up his headquarters in the big loghouse in the fort. He put a jug of good Pennsylvania whisky on the floor beside his chair. (It would dilute the ink on all the paper required to get the expedition going.) Major John Plasgrave Wyllys stamped through the barrack-rooms, harrying the work parties as they readied the place for the two hundred and thirty men of the 1st that he was expecting and whom he would command to the Miami towns. He was determined to have a unit as smart and tidy as the battalion of Continentals he had led in 1777, after the major had suffered as a prisoner of war of the British.

The summer dragged out in waiting, while the crops grew tall, grew strong. The mustered men already at Fort Washington waited in boredom for the others to arrive. In an exercise to test his men, as well as to keep the river line open upstream to Pittsburgh, General Harmar took a force to the mouth of the Scioto, which was a forward base for war parties. There were Indians there, but they fled, and Harmar marched his men back to Fort Washington. The new men, as they arrived, found the army confident after one success and swaggering toward the next.

Finally, at the end of September, the army started out for the Miami towns. Five battalions of militia broke their camp in the fields outside the fort. Of these, three battalions were Virginian Kentuckians, one was made up of Pennsylvanians, and one was the combined mounted infantry of both. The two hundred and thirty regulars of Major Wyllys had been divided into two battalions. There were one thousand four hundred and fifty-three men in all.

As they marched north, a messenger was dispatched by a roundabout, safe route to Detroit with a courteous message for the British commander. Congress considered it good, cautious diplomacy to tell the British that the considerable army bound northward through the woods meant no mischief to the good neighbor of the United States on the lakes. Governor St. Clair, who wrote the letter, stressed the punitive nature of the expedition and emphasized politely that he hoped the Crown would neither encourage nor supply the miscreant Indians in the American Northwest, Indians whose cruelties of late were an outrage on humanity. Major Patrick Murray, commanding at Detroit on the American side of the lakes, complied with the Yankee governor's request. His Indian friends had told him that the American army was eight thousand strong. Even allowing for the dramatics of Indian oratory, the number of Harmar's soldiers drew respect.

Little Turtle, war chief of the Miami, had time, and he took the opportunity, to observe the American horde as it moved north over the watershed between the Great Miami and the Maumee rivers. The Indians fell back before the oncoming Americans, but almost casually the Miami scouts stole the grazing horses from the cavalry and baggage train. Behind the screen of Indian scouts, the towns were abandoned one by one. General Harmar burned five towns, with their granaries, on the Maumee River. No Indians opposed him.

Any man who had fought in the Revolution with Dan Morgan's Virginia riflemen commanded respect as a leader on the frontier. Colonel John Hardin was such a soldier, and General Harmar agreed to let Hardin go on ahead to find the enemy and do battle. Thirty regulars of the 1st went along with the Kentuckians. At the Eel River, Little Turtle was waiting in ambush. Confidently, Colonel Hardin led the regulars across the stream and into the trap. At the first fire of the Indians, the Kentucky militia fled. Captain John Armstrong stood with the soldiers of the 1st until over half of their number were down. Then he shouted the order to break, scatter, and run. Satisfied that all his men had heard him, Armstrong turned and plunged into the river. For several hours the captain crouched in the cold water and slimy mud, his head concealed in a cluster of reeds. He could hear Little Turtle's warriors celebrating their victory on the bodies of his soldiers. When the battle site grew quiet and Armstrong could slip away, he found at the rendezvous but eight of the thirty men who had gone out; the others were dead, or soon would be, when the torturing was over.

Undaunted, Colonel Hardin petitioned General Harmar for permission to go out again, to search for the "red dogs from

hell" and to vindicate the Kentuckians who had fled. From the
high seat of command, Josiah Harmar hesitated. Before Hardin
had gone on his disastrous raid, he had destroyed five Indian
towns without battle casualties. Now those five towns had cost
the expedition twenty-two regulars dead, men he knew, and
seventy militiamen missing, presumed dead. More casualties,
and the price that Harmar must justify in his accounting to
himself, to the people, and to his government could go beyond
reason. There were other computations, too, that the commander must make. Twenty-two days had been used up in
marching to the Maumee and in destroying the towns. Two
more weeks of days would be used up in returning to Fort
Washington and closing out the ledger. Into the number of
days must be divided the supplies already consumed, to find
the rate of depletion. The remaining supplies must be
apportioned as daily rations for the return march. Another
factor to be considered was the bulk of the remaining supplies
as the weight-load capability of the remaining draught animals.
Josiah Harmar's arithmetic, addition and division and subtrac-
tion, led him to an unmistakable conclusion: to turn back.

Colonel Hardin, however, was persuasive. The precariously
balanced element of morale depended on giving the men a
chance to vindicate themselves. To leave the Miami towns
immediately after a defeat would give the Indians a confidence
which inevitably would show in an increase in the raids along
the Ohio. This would defeat the whole purpose of the
expedition. General Harmar gave his consent to attack the
Miami warriors in their camp, at the first sharp bend of the
Maumee, where it rises out of the junction of the St. Marys
and the St. Joseph rivers. Harmar attached sixty of his regulars

under Major Wyllys to Hardin's force of three hundred and forty militiamen.

The four hundred men marched off on the night of 21 September 1790 beneath shining bright stars. In the early morning Colonel Hardin divided his force. He sent Major Hill in a wide left sweep that crossed the two tributary rivers and brought him into a cutoff position above the Indians camped in the bend. Hardin himself crossed the Maumee with the regulars, militia, and cavalry. Major Hill had gained his position unnoticed by the enemy, but immediately one nervous soldier betrayed it by letting off his musket. Colonel Hardin heard the shot while he was deploying his troops for the attack. Soon a report came to him that the militiamen on the right of his line could see Indians running away through the forest. Before Hardin could issue an order the militia had started to pursue. The cavalry, too, were gone, kicking their horses into a lope, waving their long rifles, the sound of their loud halloos diminishing in the woods. The regulars held steady on the riverbank. Major Wyllys and his sixty men of the 1st Regiment took the concentrated force of the Indian attack. Little Turtle, with the main body of his warriors, swept through and over the little band of soldiers at the ford. Scarcely pausing, Little Turtle turned to pursue the militia, who still thought themselves the pursuers. Somehow, somewhere, Colonel Hardin rallied his scattered forces. Major Hill joined him. The Indians seemed everywhere and the Kentuckians were ready to run. Hardin and his officers brought the men back to the ford. There, among the bodies of the regulars, panic surmounted reason and the militia fled, splashing and stumbling through the shallow water. Indians up and down the

riverbank fired, loaded, and fired again into the headlong
plunging herd of men.

A fast-galloping cavalryman was first to arrive at Harmar's
main camp. He shouted the news to the crowd: Major Wyllys
was dead, Major Fontaine of the cavalry scalped before his
body could topple from his horse! The Maumee ford was
choked with bodies! The water ran red with blood!

Before the messenger could be brought to General Harmar,
the rot of defeat and the mold of fear had tainted the entire
army. Though the officers begged, bullied, and threatened, no
man would volunteer for a relief force. The exhausted, beaten
men straggled back to a camp that was preparing for a hasty
departure. Only Hardin was for going back with the whole
army. But Harmar had lost faith in his militia. They were the
new Kentuckians. There were few of the old stock who had
fought their Indians in their own home clearings, or rallied to
the stockades, or, in small bands, had gone north to take scalps
in revenge. The old woodswise settlers had not enlisted for
Harmar's great raid on the villagers. They had stayed at home
on the defense, expecting the Miami warriors to come to them.

After Harmar's defeat the Indians came to raid in increasing
numbers and with inflated confidence, after their successes
over Hardin. General Harmar had gone back to being colonel
of the 1st Regiment of Infantry, and with him had gone
Hardin to stand a court martial. They said it was the drink that
had undone the old soldier, though the court cleared him of
blame.

A new expedition had to be sent against the Miami towns,
and as it was his duty to his office, this task was assumed by
Governor General Arthur St. Clair.

V

General St. Clair Has Gout

Arthur St. Clair had been a British officer under Wolfe in Canada, and he had commanded Fort Ligonier in western Pennsylvania during the French and Indian War. In the War of Independence he had been one of Washington's brigadiers at the crossing of the Delaware, had lost Fort Ticonderoga to Burgoyne and had been exonerated by the ensuing court martial. He had been at Yorktown for the surrender, had been president of the Continental Congress, and had been appointed governor general of the Northwest by the President of the United States. At fifty-seven, Arthur St. Clair suffered from gout. The trip he made back over the mountains to Philadelphia in the winter of 1791 was hard on a man of the governor's age and infirmity, but it was rewarding. Secretary of War Henry Knox, whose duties included Indian affairs, and President Washington both considered him the man to lead the 1791 campaign, which would restore and re-establish the domination of the white man over the red in the American lands north of the Ohio. To mark their confidence they reinstated Arthur St. Clair in his rank of major general and gave him command of the expanded United States army. In a final quiet briefing before his return to the west, Washington and St. Clair sat long in good talk. Before taking leave of each other, Washington gave his old comrade in arms a parting admonition: "Beware of surprise." Between an order and a plea, Washington repeated, "Beware of surprise."

The enlarged United States army that Governor and Major General St. Clair would command was to include the 1st and the new 2nd Regiment of Infantry, and the Levies, volunteers for the campaign, under their own major general. One thousand Kentucky militiamen were also listed in the tables of organization that St. Clair took back with him to Pittsburgh and then downriver to expedition headquarters at Fort Washington.

A soldier is more than a number and an army more than a total figure whose pay, sustenance, arms, and clothing are authorized by a committee of men in Congress. None of the veteran officers of the Revolution, St. Clair, the commander in chief, Richard Butler, commander of the Levies and, second in command, Major Hamtramck of the regulars, and others, could consider as soldiers the men who so slowly assembled at Fort Washington that summer of 1791. The 2nd Regiment was still an unassorted mob of miscellaneous men and boys. The Levies, lured by bounty money to hire out for only six months, were hardly worth the effort that the officers must expend to give them even a semblance of a military unit. Only the men of the 1st could claim the cohesion of a regiment of soldiers. In the years of their continuity as the old First Regiment, they had drawn together in mutual respect and common purpose on which they had founded a tradition proven in disaster and accomplishment.

For St. Clair's purpose, these men plus the militia would do. This purpose, set down by Secretary Knox, was to build a series of forts from the Ohio River to the rising of the Maumee where Major Wyllys had died with so many of his regulars. Each fort, when garrisoned, would fly the starred and striped flag as a symbol of peace, friendship, and justice. The young men and their families governing and guarding and living in the loghouses would exemplify and evangelize those aims of their government. A work force of two thousand men moving through the wilderness could build the forts without too much military training. Their very number and appearance would portray an army to any Indians observing them and deter any bold attack. The garrisons left behind in the new forts as the army withdrew could train themselves into soldiers while establishing their position as friends.

If the sight of the Levies and recruits discouraged the veteran officers, the turnout of the Kentucky militia was a disappointment. Only three hundred and fifty frontiersmen answered the call, which had been reduced from one thousand to seven hundred and fifty all told. Two smaller expeditions in the spring had used up the time the militiamen could spare from their home chores. Both of their expeditions had been successful. They had burned abandoned towns along the Wabash, taken a few prisoners, and killed twenty-two warriors of "size and figure." Kentucky had had enough revenge for that year. They could not follow the U.S. regulars north, not in harvest and firewood-cutting time.

St. Clair took some consolation in the small turnout of the

militia. His army contractors, who were wont to be punctual in presenting their bills to Congress, had been overly tardy in their delivery of stores to Fort Washington. St. Clair could not have fed more than the three hundred and fifty men that Lieutenant Colonel Oldham reported on parade the morning the army moved out.

The army moved twenty miles up the Great Miami River and there stopped to build Fort Hamilton. St. Clair then struck out for the headwaters of the Wabash and the Maumee beyond. Forty-two miles further on he built Fort Jefferson in twelve days, and departed there on 24 October. St. Clair's troubles then began in earnest. The Levies' six-month enlistments were running out, and the men wanted to take their discharge where their service had begun, in taverns far to the east. Disillusioned recruits of the 2nd Regiment and the individualistic militiamen began to desert. St. Clair was forced to send back to the forts large detachments of the 1st Regiment as provosts, to round up deserters and prevent pillaging of the stores. Food was closely rationed, and a killing frost had tainted the grazing for the transport animals. St. Clair watched as a chilled and hungry army made camp on the night of 3 November, after an eight-mile march. His gout pained him as he stood looking down on the watering at the unnamed stream, the women with their buckets above, the cattle roiling the waters downstream. In bivouac that night St. Clair had only fourteen hundred men, with two hundred women cooking at the fires. Catherine Miller, with her carrot-red hair, looked like a doe in autumn as she lightly climbed up the river bank, a pail of water in each hand.

Since leaving Fort Jefferson the army had been aware that

Indians were following them along the flanks. To wander off into the woods was to be scalped, mutilated, and left to be found on the road ahead. The horse that strayed at night did not return at morning. Even the deserters left in clandestinely organized groups large enough to be safe on the back track. His request to friendly Indians for guides and scouts having been refused, St. Clair marched on blindly through the scarlet forest of autumn. He could not count the red faces that peered at his moving column or know the numbers that waited ahead. Had they been counted and tallied by their chiefs, the Indians under Little Turtle probably would have numbered two thousand or more.

Little Turtle had arisen as the great war leader of the Indians at a council called after his victories over Hardin. The Miami chief had attracted the nations to him as success draws hope. The British Deputy Agent Alexander McKee had been there to encourage the council with promises of British help and British munitions. Matthew Elliott, the British agent, had been there when the war chiefs and their young men rallied to Little Turtle that summer. He brought with him a British captain and a lieutenant to advise the red warriors in the white man's way of war. So Little Turtle had employed strategy. He refused to react to the spring raids on the upper Wabash, keeping his force intact for the main American expedition which his spies told him was mounting at Fort Washington.

For all the long summer Little Turtle held his own young men in check and kept the proud leaders of the other nations waiting with him. All the Indians, Miami, Delaware, Shawnee, Chippawa, Ottawa, Potawatomi, were eager when, in the chill of early November, Little Turtle led them out to do battle. A week earlier, he had sent out his scouts to pick up the American army as it left Fort Jefferson and to follow it, observe it, and count its numbers as it moved north. Tecumseh and his band of Shawnee scouts had followed the broad course of St. Clair's army all week. He had seen the smoke rising at the evening camp fires and in the dark he had seen the soldiers and their women silhouetted against the flames. On the night of 3 November Tecumseh and the scouts went to Little Turtle and described the lay of the Americans' camp by the little stream. Listening to the reports, Little Turtle knew that at last the enemy had arrived at the battleground.

St. Clair's gout was particularly painful on the evening of 3 November, and he had left the disposition of the camp to his commander of troops, Major General Butler. A competent and experienced officer, Butler had arrayed his regulars and Levies in two lines across the dry plateau on the near side of the stream. The guns he placed in each line. As the plateau had once been an Indian village, it was mostly cleared of trees, and gave a good field of fire. Butler put out pickets and flank guards. There was little room in the main camp, so he sent the militia, under Colonel Oldham, across the stream to set up its camp as a strong picket guard on the high ground beyond the valley, three hundred yards away.

Relieved that there had been no Indian attack while the army was strung out on the line of march, and confident in the knowledge that Indians *never* attacked an armed camp, the army retired for the night. Alert sentries throughout the night reported the presence of more Indians than usual, but no one woke the ailing general to report this fact. Before dawn the whole camp paraded, to stand by their arms until the sky was light. The time of danger and extra caution passed and the men were dismissed to breakfast, which the women were cooking at the mess fires. After breakfast, the men attended to their personal needs, to the breaking of camp, and the loading of the animals. It was then that Little Turtle attacked.

The first blow struck the detached camp of the militia. Oldham's men, scarcely waiting to pick up their weapons, raced back across the bottom land to the shelter of the main camp. The Indians followed, pausing only to fire at the running men. Some fell. By the time the U.S. artillerymen had a clear field of fire on the deserted militia camp, enemy musketfire was coming in from every quarter. Two men helped the gouty St. Clair up into an insecure seat on his horse. Butler was already in the saddle, shouting for order out of the chaos around him. Major Hamtramck, as usual sitting his horse crooked like a frog, was behind his regulars of the 2nd Regiment, yelling them into line.

The Indian fire poured into the confusion that it had created in the camp. Men running for their muskets and their gear were hit and fell sprawling. Horses, that a moment before had placidly accepted their burdens, were rearing, plunging, squealing, stampeding beasts, trampling the fallen, knocking down those in their headlong way. The bodies of women lay rumpled on half-rolled blankets and among the overturned cookpots. Men taking position in the slowly forming firing line were hit by balls of soft British lead. The Americans had begun to fire back. The Indians took up more concealed positions. Those within range concentrated their fire on the exposed artillerymen serving their guns. Captain James Bradford fell as the Indians picked off the officers and the gun sergeants. One by one the guns, without living men to work them, fell silent.

For three hours the musketfire continued in and all around the camp on the low plateau. The Indians, who charged in small howling groups, were driven back by the soldiers who now in desperation had steadied down to defense. Still the murderous, accurately searching musketfire poured in. General Butler was hit, hard wounded but alive. Three times General St. Clair had crashed down in a blaze of pain when his horse was killed under him. His coarse coat was rent in many places by balls that his imposing white-haired figure had attracted. Half his army was dead or badly wounded. Somehow, St. Clair and his officers concentrated the remaining men for a charge. They picked a quarter from which the Indian fire appeared weakest and, charging, broke through. They gained the road and ran back toward Fort Jefferson. The pathetic sound of dwindling musketfire from the wounded left in the camp only increased the pace of panic. In the forefront of the flight ran Catherine Miller, her long red hair streaming out behind her. Adjutant General Sargent followed the bright banner of the racing girl's hair. Somewhere in the ruck of the beaten army its gouty general clung to the back of a led packhorse.

On the high ground beside the stream, Little Turtle's Indians finished their morning's work. They killed the wounded, plundered the dead, and rounded up the cattle. Simon Girty, the renegade American who ran with, and today had led, the Wyandot, found the wounded Richard Butler and dispatched him at leisure. As the Indians had done with the other bodies, Girty forced open the dead general's mouth and crammed it with earth, Indian earth from Indian land. Let the white man eat the earth for which he was so greedy. The Indians would give him no more than a mouthful.

Fourteen hundred men and some two hundred women had made camp on the night of 3 November. Nine hundred, including fifty-six of the women, did not return to the haven of Fort Jefferson. The soldiers of the 1st Regiment who were there to stop deserters now took in the refugees. As expeditiously as possible the regulars passed the remnants of St. Clair's army back down the line to Fort Washington. The Levies, their service expired, scattered to their more distant haunts. The recruits of the 2nd Regiment were sent to cantonments for hard training into soldiers. Arthur St. Clair went to the inevitable court martial of a defeated general. Three hundred good regulars of the 1st Regiment of Infantry stood alone on the frontier, waiting for the raids that were certain to follow Little Turtle's second year of victories.

VI

The Legion of the United States

Ensign William Henry Harrison, so very new to the life and duties of a soldier in the army in the west, heard the retold tale of St. Clair's defeat and rout. As he practiced his close order drill, the lessons of defeat were instilled into him with each step of the maneuver. In off-duty hours he heard the stories of Indian ways and details of past raids and ambushes. When he took the guard or the detail, first with another officer, then, one proud day, alone, he learned to expect the sudden rush of moccasined feet, and he walked wary of the ambush.

There was no soldier or settler on the frontier who had not heard the eyewitness account of how the Indians liked to torture their white captives slowly with fire. All the horrible details of burning at the stake were confirmed that winter following St. Clair's defeat. The Indians spent all one day killing Abner Hunt, while a helpless garrison watched from a besieged blockhouse. Hunt suffered out his death too far from the fort to receive the mercy bullet from his friends. Yet he was near enough for his screams to be heard behind the log walls. That incident occurred at Dunlap Station, not far from Fort Washington.

Some of the white captives escaped, to bring back tales of torment in the forest and slavery in the Indian towns. Others were bartered among the warriors for silver medallions or sold to white traders for strong drink to satisfy the Indians' craving. One girl, Dolly Fleming, seized from a flatboat in 1790, was rescued by a compassionate chief who sent her home in disguise.

The fighting was sharp that winter and spring of 1791–92. Even Pittsburgh, the Ohio River metropolis, had its scare. Kentucky, on the eve of achieving statehood, was penetrated by marauding war parties which struck deeply and at will. On 1 June 1792, Governor Isaac Shelby's inaugural address as first governor of the fifteenth state was interrupted by a skirmish with Indians in the environs of the town where he spoke. Rangers on defensive patrol took the settlers' revenge on Indian bands returning north. Scouts were kept out to warn communities of Indians in the neighborhood and to rally the people to the communal fort or blockhouse.

No one warned John Merrill and his wife on Christmas Eve 1791. He was wounded in the first attack, but with his wife's help he made it into the cabin and barred the door. The howling Indians were outside, chopping at the door. John lay all but helpless by the fireplace, while his wife stood beside the door, the axe in her hands. A board gave way and the Indians began crawling through to get at the wounded man. As each Indian straightened up, Mrs. Merrill swung the axe. She killed four men before the others drew back. Next, the Indians tried coming down the wide chimney. Mrs. Merrill snatched her

feather bolster from the bed and threw it on the fire. Two
Indians, overcome by smoke, tumbled down inside the cabin.
John Merrill found the strength to brain them with a stick of
firewood. The other Indians went away.

The United States army, as far as possible, remained aloof
from the raids that thundered or distantly rumbled around
their base at Fort Washington. Their mission was to maintain
the line of forts that General St. Clair had erected into the
Indian country. The Indians, however, did not leave the
bluecoats entirely alone. They watched the supply road
between Forts Washington and Jefferson and Forts Jefferson
and Hamilton. Once, in the spring, the warriors felt themselves strong enough to attack a convoy near Fort Jefferson.
They killed sixteen soldiers. A search party found the bodies.

After St. Clair's departure, Colonel James Wilkinson
commanded the U.S. troops in the west. He was a latent
traitor and the type of westerner whom Washington dreaded
to find in the new land. At the time he took command,
Wilkinson was undecided as to where his best interests lay. He
was also working underground, already in fee to the Spanish
governor in Louisiana and seeking contact with the British in
Canada. Both his promotion to brigadier general and the U.S.
government's policy for the Northwest Territory for the year
1792 fostered Wilkinson's own ends. Because of his new rank
he demanded and received better pay from the Spanish
governor. And because the government in Philadelphia was
seeking an Indian peace through negotiation, Wilkinson was
ordered to avoid offensive action by his soldiers and to keep
angry Kentuckians from carrying their reprisals north of the
Ohio River. In February Wilkinson ordered a force to the site

of St. Clair's defeat to find the remains of the dead and give them decent burial. No one, Indians, British, Americans, or Spaniards, could consider such an expedition aggressive. In May Wilkinson thought the time ripe to send his own personal ambassador, Sergeant Reuben Reynolds, to the British in Detroit. Reynolds successfully made the dangerous passage through the Indian country in peace. The government's ambassadors, going openly to parley with the chiefs, were not as fortunate as the sergeant. Colonel John Hardin, the principal in Harmar's double defeat, was tomahawked. Major Alexander Trueman, a casualty of St. Clair's battle and Hardin's co-ambassador, was found murdered in the woods. In the mounting temper of the frontier the two deaths were blamed on the British. The indignation of the western people began to be heard in the Congress of the United States.

Until the great migration year of 1788, the settling of the west was a state affair, concerning only Pennsylvania, Virginia, and the Carolinas. New England, ever loud in the parliament of states, had little stake in the new lands beyond the mountains. The generation in power in all the Atlantic states from Delaware to Massachusetts' Maine province were well removed in time as well as distance from the facts of an Indian raid. Not until the early 1790's did the townsman of Boston or the farmer of Connecticut have the Indian way of death brought into his painted clapboard house. Then a young New England man who went to Ohio with his bride, a girl from the same town, had been raided and scalped. The grandparents never saw the grandchild born in the plundered cabin. Their former neighbor from down the road had gone west too. He had been burned out, his cattle stolen.

Self-interest joined humane sympathy in drawing the easterners' indignant attention to the problems of the western settlers. Many of the land companies promoting the migration were funded in the east. Their directors were usually so eminent that, in spite of some financial scandals, they claimed the attention and rhetoric of New England congressmen. The advent of senators and representatives of seventy-five thousand Kentuckians to the chambers of Congress also generated attention to the west among the lawmakers and the appropriators of budget monies. The raid on the Massachusetts settlement at Big Bottom, following Harmar's defeat, so moved Congress that it gave Washington the 2nd Regiment of Infantry. St. Clair's disaster, the continuing raids, and the murder of the ambassadors gave Washington the Legion of the United States and a universal militia service law embracing all men between eighteen and sixty.

Secretary of War Knox fathered the Legion system. As Washington's general of artillery he had observed the work and the effect of the Legion as organized by both the British and the French commanders. As with the old Roman Legion, their contemporary counterpart was a mixed force of all arms, horse, foot, and artillery, balanced according to where and how it must fight. The combat team of regimental strength made up of all arms seemed well suited to the conditions of a war in the Northwest Territory. Knox's extensive reading and study of Julius Caesar's campaigns in Gaul and Britain bore out the analogy. Roman Legions had kept back the barbarians along the River Rhine. American Legions could keep the Indians north of the Ohio. In Britain the *castras* had been fortified centers of Roman life in a wilderness full of hostile savages.

The Legionnaires marching the Roman roads had slapped out beneath their sandaled feet the beat of civilization that was heard and heeded by the painted tribes of Britain. Forts and roads were already a fact of United States policy in the Indian land below the Great Lakes. The comparison with Rome's empirical expansion held another bonus for the studious Secretary of War. The name "Legion of the United States" offered a happy compromise to a Congress that feared the word "Army," yet had to provide protection for its constituents in a warring west.

The Legion of the United States was formed by Knox to fight in the river maze of the Ohio Valley, to erect and man the forts, build and patrol the roads between, and give the land peace under American law and custom. There were four legions, in the old Roman sense, that made up the Legion of the United States. Each, called a sub-legion, was composed of one thousand eighty men, infantry, artillery, and cavalry, under the command of a brigadier general. The major general commanding the whole would thus have four complete armies, already assembled and organized, who could march off in four directions at once. No longer would the general have to assemble his three tools of war: horse, foot, and guns. The Legion gave him a composite tool, ready to march and work alone.

The man that Washington chose to create and then to command the Legion was "Mad Anthony Wayne." The nickname, given in affection, had been earned at that time of battle when the planning and the maneuvering is done and the example of leadership tips the balance to success. The madness of Anthony Wayne had been witnessed on Revolutionary

War battlefields from Canada to Georgia, from 1776 to 1781. But the fury and the madness of General Anthony Wayne hid the basic caution of the man. As the successful farmer that he was, Wayne had kept his scythe sharp, his harrow bright and his planting carefully arranged in anticipation of the harvest. When Washington called Wayne from his farm in March 1792, he was calling the tried cultivator of soldiers as well as the bold madman in battle.

The new commander of the fighting strength of the United States of America was forty-seven, and as handsome a senior major general as he had been a junior. An old wound he had taken at Stony Point and the hardships of old campaigns hampered him physically, but his will was as untarnished as the gold medal he had won with his wound. His dress was as elegant as ever as he set out for Pittsburgh followed by the scruffy lot of men—squeezed by recruiting sergeants from old tavern mops—who were the soldiers of the 3rd and 4th sub-legions. The 1st and 2nd Regiments of Infantry, with their guns and new-found mounts, were already calling themselves sub-legions.

General Wayne marched his recruits the whole long way, from east to west, across his native Pennsylvania. Fewer arrived than had set out. The weak of body and will had fallen by the wayside. The remainder would make good soldiers of the Legion. If the men anticipated the delights of Pittsburgh at the end of the weary march, their general disappointed them. With scarcely a whiff of the whisky or a whistle at the girls, Wayne's men were marched through the town. At a pre-selected place downriver the general had them build their camp in the Roman manner: fortified, neat, and orderly. Anthony Wayne dubbed the place Legionville. There he created the Legion of the United States.

Wayne had two uninterrupted years to train his men. The hostile Indians paid the settlements little attention during the raiding season of 1792. They were busy moving their scattered towns northward, into a concentration that was in no way a withdrawal, in the fertile Maumee Valley. The move of the Miami and the Shawnee brought them ever closer to British influence and to the bounties they might expect from the Crown. An armistice followed this period of quiet as Britain and America and some twenty-eight Indian nations prepared for a great council to be held in the spring of 1793. Angry altercations over the site and protocol foredoomed the council before it met. Joseph Brant, the great Mohawk leader, tried to save the conference, but he could do nothing, though he traveled to London and to Philadelphia on behalf of peace for his people. Joseph Brant was now *Old* Joseph Brant, and the young leaders could not see his version of Indian unity, or hear his logic on co-existence. Brant was held suspect, too, by the new lieutenant governor of the recently created Province of Upper Canada, which embraced the Great Lakes. Lieutenant Governor John Graves Simcoe took to his frontier province a hatred of Yankees learned as the British colonel commanding a Loyalist Corps in the rebellion that he never acknowledged as a revolution. Simcoe continued in the old hostility as he administered the governor general's policy of fostering an Indian buffer state in the American treaty lands south and west of Upper Canada.

George Washington, receiving Brant with respect, approached the council with practicality and the faint hope of a

sound peace. The United States was yet too young and insecure to enter into another war. Like Simcoe, Washington
needed time to absorb the growing western territories, and by
talk he could gain time for General Wayne to build the Legion
as the solid answer to the Indian menace. The Anglo-Indian
questions of 1792 and 1793 were not Washington's only problems in the lands of the west. The two-year-old state of Kentucky was flaunting its newly accepted adulthood with an attitude of jejeune independence. A "citizen" Genêt, who was
ambassador from Republican France of the Reign of Terror,
had come among the Kentuckians to provoke violent revolution from Kentucky and Tennessee into the Spanish king's domain on the Gulf of Mexico. Kindred souls raised an army of
liberation on the aroused frontier. One arm of the invading
force seized a base on the Ohio River. Hurriedly General
Wayne assembled a force of the Legion downstream of the filibusters to deny them access to the Mississippi River and New
Orleans. Fervor cooled and the "liberators" went home.

Small leaders are never lacking in a time of change and a
place of rapid growth. While the Kentuckians were listening
to the trained voice from France, the Scotch and Irish in far
western Pennsylvania were brewing their own private griev-
ance against an absentee, meddlesome, greedy, and probably
teetotal government. Congress had imposed an excise tax on
whisky. The Pennsylvanians made fine whisky, strong
whisky. The more they made the more they drank, and the
stronger the Scots and Irish of the Monongahela felt about the
tax. The active phase of the Whisky Rebellion did not break
out until Wayne and his Legion, drinkers of western whisky,
were far away. Washington had to call out thirteen thousand

militiamen before the brew-up cooled and the excise tax was accepted, albeit grudgingly.

Against this background of rumblings of unrest, "Mad Anthony Wayne" drilled and drilled and drilled his sub-legions. He had his usual success. British Deputy Indian Agent McKee, at his house at the Maumee Rapids, complimented the Legion by his concern about its employment. The Kentucky filibusters lauded it by loudly jeering at the Legion's discipline, appearance, and self-esteem. They put Wayne down as a sick old drunkard. The Indians, who watched from the forest, also underestimated Wayne. They gave him the nickname "Black-snake"—a harmless, cautious snake with no more than a threatening hiss.

In the fall of 1793 the Indians confirmed the nickname. They attacked a convoy, completely routing the ninety-man escort, and killed fourteen Legionaries and two good young officers. Wayne took the defeat as an excuse for more drill. By then he had moved the Legion from the training camp at Legionville. After a pause at Fort Washington, where the town of Cincinnati was building up, Wayne had moved up St. Clair's access road. Six miles beyond Fort Jefferson, he camped at a place he named for General Nathanael Greene, which became Greenville. While there he lost the convoy. On the day before Christmas Wayne was ill. But he left his bed to march on with his troops to the place where St. Clair had met defeat. He marked the spot with a fort, which he named "Recovery." There he recovered the guns St. Clair had lost, finding them where Little Turtle had buried them. To Wayne, winter quarters meant drill and work and discipline. It was thus he had held together a faction-riven army at Ticonderoga in the

horrible winter of 1776–77. At Fort Recovery there was main-
tenance and gun drill for the gunners, horsemanship and pursuit with the long saber for the dragoons. Riflemen skirmished
and refined their aim at the mark. The infantry charged and
charged again with the bayonet, which since before Stony
Point had been Wayne's favorite weapon. General Wayne
personally trained and exercised his own small staff. Among
the more promising young men of the general's family was
William Henry Harrison, now a lieutenant seconded from the
1st sub-legion.

It was a short winter quarters for the Legion of the United
States. The sugar sap would soon run in northern Ohio. The
leafing out would follow quickly. Wayne was not far from the
Maumee River, the place he had chosen for the campaign of
1794.

VII

At Fallen Timbers on the Maumee

The old fort and town of Detroit was on the American side of
the river. Everyone living there in 1794 was as much aware of
that fact of political geography as of the fact that the flag on the
bastion was the Union Jack.

The borderline that ran down the middle of the Detroit
River had been drawn there in 1783 in France, by wise men
seeking a peaceful solution to the War of American Independence. The paragraph of the Treaty of Versailles which defined
the American Northwest, and which placed Detroit in the
United States, had been a stroke of diplomatic genius by the
American negotiators, regretted almost immediately by the
British signatories. The Crown, also being possessed of
nimble-witted diplomats, protested an American interpretation
of one of the terms of the peace by remaining in the
Northwest. For ten years the men of reason argued their
points. The Americans meanwhile built their strength to force
the British out of Detroit, and the British, without military or
civil strength to go to the Ohio River, sponsored the Indian

nations in their efforts to keep their homeland, which lay in the disputed territory.

In 1794, the eleventh year of the dispute, a crisis was imminent. The governor general of all Canada, Lord Dorchester, had advised and urged Little Turtle and other chiefs who came to see him in Quebec to draw the line between America and Canada on the Ohio. To underline his intimation of armed help for the Indians, the governor general ordered his lieutenant governor in Upper Canada to rebuild and man with soldiers old Fort Miami, which stood at the rapids of the Maumee River. For the two years that he had been in his province Lieutenant Governor Simcoe had concentrated on its military readiness. He had organized an army of some four hundred men to which he had given the name of his old Loyalist Corps, the Queen's Rangers. The duties of the new Rangers were twofold: to defend against American attack as soldiers on land and as sailors on the lakes, and to build roads of movement, called streets, across the province. Simcoe was now ready with the means to implement the governor general's orders. Fort Miami was rebuilt, cannon were mounted, and Major William Campbell was given the place in charge. Lieutenant Colonel Richard England commanded British regulars and Canadian militia at Detroit, forty miles away. Lieutenant Governor Simcoe was at his capital, across the length of Lake Erie. He was raising troops, finding artillery, and gathering a fleet so that he himself could actively defend the bold outpost on the Maumee and protect Detroit, the supposed objective of the Yankees' expedition in 1794.

The Indian nations from north and east and west sent war parties to the assembly with the Miami and Cherokee on the

Maumee. The governor general's encouragement had made the warriors eager to fight. Simcoe, England, Campbell, and McKee promised active support. Simpler men in and around Detroit had daubed their white skins with paint and attached themselves to bands at the rendezvous. Only Little Turtle was hesitant. He had taken Wayne's measure, and he realized that the new white general had the cunning as well as the caution of the blacksnake. He suspected that Wayne had the fangs of the rattlesnake. But other leaders wanted to pluck the eagle feathers of victory and they scorned Little Turtle. Nation after nation struck out from the dance fires alone to hunt the white man's road. They had small success. The biggest concentration attacked Fort Recovery, on the hallowed ground of the victory over St. Clair. They attacked all the day of 30 June and far into the night, killing soldiers who were firing at them from the loopholes. Little Turtle counted the horses captured and weighed them against the Indians killed that day. He saw more dead than in the November battle of 1791. That night Little Turtle persuaded the other chiefs to give up the hopeless siege and return to the rendezvous on the Maumee. Some of the war parties never bothered to return to the Indians' base camp; others paused only long enough to get food for the long journey to their homes. One battle made a whole campaign for the Indians, and Little Turtle and McKee, the Deputy Indian Agent, were hard put to keep half of the two thousand warriors who had first come to the rendezvous. Little Turtle and the depleted war party waited through the warm July for Wayne to come out of his forts. Only by surprise attacks on the march or in open bivouacs had red warriors ever defeated white soldiers.

General Anthony Wayne did not leave his forts until 28
July. By then he had all his supplies up and his wagons and
pack animals ready to move them forward. The detachments
from the sub-legions had been assigned to guard the forts
which were strung out along almost a hundred miles of road to
the Ohio River. All Wayne's officers knew the plan of march.
All understood their general's plan of defense and attack:
charge with the bayonet.

The Legion of the United States had never recruited up to
its full authorized strength. With all the detachments to the
forts, the sub-legions ready to march in July 1794 numbered in
all but fifteen hundred men. But the four fingers, infantry,
artillery, cavalry and riflemen, closed into a strong right fist, if
a small one.

Wayne's left hook was the sixteen hundred mounted
riflemen from Kentucky who had joined the army at the sharp
end of the road on 26 July. They rode into Greenville in
companies and regiments behind their leader, the Indian
fighter Major General Charles Scott. The two generals
greeted each other with respect and friendship. Both had
attained general's rank in the Revolution, though while
Wayne had compounded his fame and reputation, Scott had
been a paroled prisoner from 1777 to the end of the war. In
Kentucky, Charles Scott had been one of the statemakers, and
as militia leader he had successfully rallied veteran frontiersmen in maneuver and pursuit during the dark days after
Harmar's and St. Clair's disasters. While Wayne was pains-
takingly marshaling his Legion, Scott's high reputation as a
soldier had brought out the sixteen hundred best fighting men
of Kentucky to work with the Legion. The companies of

mounted men with their clean brown rifles fell into the march
north on the left flank of their comrades of the Legion. They,
like the U.S. regulars, knew where they were going, what they
were to do, and, experienced under command, they knew how
to act and react to emergency.

The army marched to the northeast from Fort Recovery.
The weather was hot and the mosquitoes plagued the men of
the Legion, sweating as they tramped along in their uniforms.
They grumbled as troops grumble, envying the Kentucky men
riding, marching, or leading their horses in a comfortable
variety of woods dress. But uniforms were Wayne's way and
in his dress he himself was as immaculate as he was correct. By
the color of the horsehair and variegated plumes in their caps,
or by the plumes alone if they wore the new roached hats,
Wayne could tell at a glance to which sub-legion each man or
officer belonged. The neat blue coats faced with white marked
the Legion as an entity to be recognized and respected
anywhere.

The men marched by day through the hills of western Ohio.
They marched in an order precise as their dress and discipline,
with cordons of guards at the front, at the rear, and on the
flanks. Each cordon had increasing resilience toward the
center, where the main body, Kentuckians on the left, regulars
on the right, marched with the baggage and guns. In the
afternoon all halted to build the night's camp, secure and
fortified, as the Roman Legions had done before them.

Beyond the moving mass of the army the wide-ranging
scouts and spies roamed. At times the point men of the army
would find a spy waiting in the woods ahead. He would
quickly be passed through the cordons to where the spymaster,

Ephraim Kirby, rode close to Anthony Wayne. Under "Captain" Kirby were friendly Indians from the southern mountains, who had old hurts to revenge on the Indians above the Ohio. The true spies were those odd men betwixt red and white, who had the cautious curiosity of the white-tailed deer and the solitary urge of the hunting great cat. One of them, May, was a pathfinder. It was he whom the army found staked out in the road, his heart ripped out and missing, a warning mark cut into his left breast. One spy, Miller, did general work, and as needed he could make contact with the enemy Indians, who in turn were scouting the soldiers marching toward the Maumee. Close to General Wayne in his tent of an evening or when plans were discussed and decided was William Wells, once of Kentucky but until recently a Miami warrior. Wells had been captured by the Indians at the age of twelve. He had been raised to manhood among them and had fought Harmar and St. Clair at the side of his wife's father, Little Turtle. Wells's return to the world of the white man, his going back to his own people, provided General Wayne an intimate view of his enemy.

The great encampment of Little Turtle's warriors stood where the Au Glaise River enters the Maumee. Early in August Wayne's army was on the upper tributaries of the Au Glaise. On 8 August Wayne ordered all the guns cleared and reloaded. He enjoined even stricter security for the next day's move and he issued a gill of whisky to each man. Walking about the camp at the time of the evening meal, Wayne promised the men green corn and fresh squash in the Indian towns.

Five miles above the mouth of the Au Glaise, the army came

to the first of the cornfields. The stalks were up, the ears tasseling out, and the long green runners of the squash brightened the ground between the rows. The soldiers marched on, their spirits lifted, to the rich beautiful country. There were no Indians. Scouts who were first into the empty towns reported that the Indians had made a hasty departure. The men had their vegetables that night.

They built a loghouse and surrounded it with pickets, giving it the name of Fort Defiance. It would guard the Maumee ford, which the pioneers had made usable for the wagons by cutting back the banks and laying a corduroy road down to the water's edge. On 11 August the army crossed over and resumed their march. Wayne moved slowly but purposefully down the Maumee. He was expecting some word from Little Turtle, asking for peace. Miller, the spy, made the contact and brought the flag of truce to Wayne. The Indians wanted Wayne to halt his advance while the talks were initiated. The American general, while willing to talk, preferred to stop at a place of his own choosing. That place was a strategic knoll above the Maumee Rapids. There the army built Fort Deposit as a place to leave its heavy baggage while the soldiers fought if necessary or stayed while Wayne negotiated favorably from the strength of their arms.

Little Turtle had been taken by surprise by General Wayne's march down the Au Glaise. He had expected "Blacksnake" to go directly to a confrontation with the British at the fort below the Maumee Rapids. Little Turtle had ordered the hasty evacuation of the Au Glaise towns, while he hurried away to confer with Colonel Richard England, the British commander at Detroit. When the Miami chief went

before the colonel he held doubts that the British had the intent
or the ability to fight beside the Indians, but Colonel England
encouraged the chief with immediate action. A levy of troops
went at once to reinforce the garrison at Fort Miami. McKee,
the Indian Agent, assured Little Turtle that the warriors who
had gone home would return. Colonel England told the Miami
that the lieutenant governor himself was coming from Niagara
in a fleet of boats crowded with soldiers. Both the Englishmen
urged Little Turtle to go back to the Maumee and gain time
by a truce. Ten days would be enough. His doubts about
British help removed, and his Indian allies elated, Little Turtle
returned to initiate the false truce and to prepare an ambush.
On 16 August the Indian ambassador made contact with the
American spy, Miller. On 18 August all the warriors were set
in their places of ambush.

The Indians lay or crouched in among the fallen trunks and
branches of great hardwood trees, felled in a swath of
destruction by a recent tornado. From their hides the warriors
could see across the plain to the Maumee River, angling
toward the line of fallen timber. The American bluecoats and
the Kentuckians marching down the river plain must compress
their front in order to pass between the water's edge and the
first of the toppled trees. In doing so, a long flank would be
exposed to the fire of Indian muskets. The Indian right flank,
where the great windfall ended, was too far away for the
Americans to march around. At the point in the tangled trunks
from which the trap would be triggered, Tecumseh waited.
No Indian in the Northwest was better qualified by experience
or restraint to gauge the moment to spring the ambush than
the Shawnee. With his scouts around him, Tecumseh waited.

At the river end of the line, Turkey Foot with his Ottawa was also waiting. Antoine Laselle also waited, and to pass the time, he sang *voyageur* songs in his native French. A thousand others waited. They waited all day of 18 August and all of the following day. Their battle tension softened with the erosion of the passing hours. The rust of delay dulled the keen edge of their confidence.

In its own deliberate time, Wayne's army left Fort Deposit at seven o'clock on the morning of 20 August. The Legion marched on the right, as usual, with the riverbank close by. The men carried light packs only and their bayonets were honed sharp and bright. The faithless Wilkinson, subdued for the moment under Wayne's control, lead the massed sub-legions. The main body of the Kentuckians marched with Colonel Levi Todd on the left of the regulars. Though the army was still on the river plain, the ground was less spongy away from the water and gave better footing for the horses. General Scott, with the best mounted of the Kentucky riflemen, rode on the left flank. The day was fair, the pace slow through green meadowland, relieved by tall shade trees and cool copses.

General Wayne rode well forward where he could see and judge the springing of the ambush he expected. From where he rode among his men, General Wayne could direct the battle as it developed, and if his "Madness" were needed, he could lead the charge. Had Lieutenant Harrison, the other two aides, and the doctor had their way, Anthony Wayne would have missed the march. The general's bad leg was considerably swollen that day. He could not ride, the aides protested. He had issued detailed orders to competent commanders. He was not needed up front. But Wayne would not listen, and while they brought his horse he had the doctor bind his leg from ankle to thigh. The three aides hoisted their general into the saddle, mounted themselves and fell in behind. He rode awkwardly, his bandaged leg sticking out, but the men, regulars and militia, walked or rode straighter as Anthony Wayne passed them on his way to the front; he was more man than most men.

Tecumseh lay his musket's sight on the horseman at the edge of the trees. The Kentuckian was still too far away. So was the bluecoated infantry company down by the river. To his right a young Shawnee with an arrow nocked to his bow string was watching the chief. Elsewhere, near at hand, Tecumseh could hear other Indians rustling into new positions. There was the double click of a gun hammer being drawn back to the cock. A company of bluecoated infantry, the flank guard, was coming into view, the line of march oblique to Tecumseh's front. The officer in front was pointing toward the line of fallen trees at which the marching men were all looking. The high sun glinted on the long bayonets as the men turned to see where their officer pointed. A company of mounted men trotted out of a little wood, interposed them- selves between the infantry and Tecumseh, and reined into a walk. On the Shawnee's left all the way to the river American troops were drawing close to the line of fallen timbers. In front of the Shawnee scouts, the horsemen were in bowshot range of the young warrior kneeling beside his chief. Tecumseh picked his target, sighted on the man and fired. All along the ambush line muskets went off and arrows arced across the sky. From behind the Indian fireline, long howling war whoops rose from the second line of Indians and, still further back, from the third. Some Indians crowded forward from the rear to fire at the disordered Americans. Tecumseh, ramming home a new load of shot, could not find the horseman at whom he had fired. Men and horses were milling about in complete confusion. The general motion of the plunging, kicking mass was away from the Shawnee. Tecumseh went back to the work of firing, reloading, and firing again.

Captain Howell Lewis, with his company of the 3rd sub-legion, had been marching flank guard when the company of mounted rifles had trotted up. They had taken a position between his men and the line of fallen timber that angled across his front and that, seemingly, crowded the horsemen into his company even as he seemed to be crowding into the main body of the army, marching on his right. The mounted men took the first sudden blast of the Indians' fire. They had been ordered by General Scott to fall back at the first fire, draw off to the left and reassemble with Scott. But, startled and wounded by the suddenness of the attack, the horses panicked. They kicked, reared, plunged, bucked, and backed off to run, while their struggling riders fought to stay in the saddle, wrenched at the reins and sawed at the bits, trying to get their mounts under control. Shouting, cursing, and snorting, the whole seething mass slammed into Howell's ordered ranks of infantry. The Legion broke and ran before the tangled onslaught. Forty yards behind the mess of men and horses, Captain Howell was waving his sword and shouting to his men to rally to him. They came, bruised, bumped, and battered. Grumbling, they reformed their ranks. The horsemen, too, had regained control over their mounts and were galloping off to their rendezvous with General Scott. A few dead lay crumpled between the company of the 3rd sub-legion and the smoke drifting up all along the line of fallen trees. Some of the wounded walked toward Howell's line, helped by riflemen who had been thrown from horses now running wildly, stirrup leathers flapping, after the retreating cavalry.

Under the supervising eye of Wayne, Brigadier General Wilkinson was executing the standing order of the Legion: charge with the bayonet. There was a minimum of shouted orders and little fuss as the files performed the often practiced ritual of movement to change their front. Almost casually, the order to charge was given and the long blue line of infantry stepped off in the steady measure of a walk. Only Captain Lewis's company ran. In the confusion with the horses they had lost time. Now they ran forward to catch up and take their place on the end of the line. With the 1st, 2nd, the 4th, and the others of the 3rd sub-legion, Lewis's men brought their muskets down to the charge. Pressing now behind the slim hard points of their bayonets, the Legion went in among the fallen timbers.

The Indians had kept up their fire as the Americans advanced. Though they had seen men stumble and fall, the blue line of soldiers tramped steadily forward. As the silent line drew nearer, the Indian barrage of musketfire and arrows quickened and grew erratic; it also became less accurate. As the line approached still more closely, the warriors fell back deeper and deeper into the great windfall—to gain time to reload their muskets or to fit new strings to their bows. Some of the Indians were in full retreat. At the river end of the line, Turkey Foot jumped up on a big rock, the better to shout encouragement to his Ottawa. A rifleman took aim, fired, and brought the chief down. The Ottawa warriors fled, and the

U.S. troops moved into the gap between the fallen trees and the river.

Tecumseh and his Shawnee scouts were gone from their vantage place, as were the Indians ranged just behind them. Very few stood to meet the bayonets of Wayne's soldiers. Inside the blow-down, the trim blue line became ragged, moving forward slowly and jerkily, but still under the control of the officers. The bayonet charge was over. Now the men of the infantry were permitted to fire their muskets at targets of opportunity. The battle line moved forward through the zone of fallen timbers, probing under the big trunks and searching around the torn roots for men in hiding. So they found Antoine Laselle, his white skin showing under the paint and dress of a warrior. A soldier with a cocked musket marched the renegade back at bayonet-point. At the far edge of the fallen timbers the infantry halted. Their work was done.

In the river plain beyond, Wayne's dragoons and Scott's mounted rifles had begun their part of the job. The cavalry of the Legion, swords drawn, had passed around the river flank where Turkey Foot's body lay beside the big rock. Scott had led his horsemen in a wild ride around the fallen timbers and back onto the river plain. There in the meadowland the combined cavalry chased the Indians, flushed from their cover by the infantry. The Kentucky men fired and reloaded from the saddle: the dragoons, sabers swinging, ran down the fleeing warriors. Short of the British fort, plainly marked by its Union Jack, on the left bank of the river, the cavalry charge halted. Safely out of range of the fort's cannon, the mounted men rested their horses, tightened the loosened tack, and saw to their weapons.

From where they had halted, Scott and his officers could see the gate of the fort. It was closed. Outside, trying to get into the shelter of the fort was a mob of Indians. But the gate remained closed. Redcoated soldiers could be seen manning the wall. Slowly the mass of Indians broke up to continue their retreat downriver. The last Indian turned to leave. In the distance he could see the Yankee horsemen, the enemy who had beaten him in battle. Near by was the house of his sworn friend and beholden ally, shut fast against him.

The refusal of the British to fight with and for their friends was the Indian nations' second defeat that day. Beaten in fair fight at Fallen Timbers, and beaten in spirit at the closed gate of Fort Miami, Little Turtle was ready to ask an American peace in the Northwest. The other chiefs could be brought around to the Miami's way of thinking.

VIII

Peace After Greenville

One battle does not win a war. A single victory is not a final defeat. After his victorious battle at Fallen Timbers, Anthony Wayne stayed in the valley of the Maumee to finish the war on the Indians and to convince them of their defeat. By his very presence, he offered his army for a second attack in case the Indians still doubted its invincibility. By laying waste the Indian cornland all up and down the valley, Wayne destroyed the Indians' ability and will to fight again another year. Before he left the Maumee at the end of October, he had convinced the nations that Americans could go where they wished and do as they wished in the Northwest.

The British, however, remained on American land. Only forty miles from Wayne's camp below the Maumee Rapids, Britain ruled Detroit as her own. In plain sight of the Legions' pickets, the Union Jack above Fort Miami flapped in the summer breeze. Through a spyglass General Wayne could see the cannon, run out, their round mouths taunting him. Although the guns remained silent, quill pens scratched furiously over paper as General Wayne and Major Campbell spat and snarled at each other. The exchange of bombast was as futile as it was personally satisfying. Campbell, penned inside the walls of his insignificant fort, waiting for Simcoe to come with his army, had neither the rank nor the temerity to commit Britain to a war. Wayne's orders emphatically restricted him to a campaign against the Indian nations. Both the commanders confronting each other on the bank of that remote river knew that the Northwest question had to be decided by far loftier authority than theirs. Even as the messengers with white flags flying and drums beating marched back and forth between the fort and the camp, the camp and the fort, the question was being answered in distant London. John Jay, the jurist, concluded his special embassy to the British Crown in November 1794. By the terms of Jay's Treaty, Detroit would be turned over to the Americans on 1 June 1796.

At twelve noon on 23 August each of the Legion's sixteen guns tolled three shots in farewell to the forty-four American dead. Then the American army marched back upriver. For eight miles around Fort Miami the Americans had laid waste the land, and on the march to Fort Defiance they continued to scorch the earth. For seventeen days General Wayne kept the army at Fort Defiance. He gave the troops two days to clean up, then he inspected them. The rest of the time he worked them and drilled them to polish off the rough edges of sloppiness that erode a victorious army. By 12 September General Wayne considered his soldiers to be ready, and he gave the order to sharpen all axes. Even the dullest soldier knew that "sharpen axes" meant that the army was going on, not back to the permanent camp of the Legion at Greenville.

Wayne took the men forty-seven miles up the Maumee to the Miami villages near the ford where the old 1st Regiment of Infantry had taken the heavy losses at Harmar's defeat. There, on five hundred cleared acres at the first sweeping bend of the Maumee, General Wayne built his fort. Fort Wayne was built as a major post to hold and dominate the source of five river roads. The Maumee River led directly to Lake Erie, the St. Joseph to Lake Michigan. The longest portage was to the Illinois, which flowed into the Mississippi above the Missouri River. The Wabash curved westward through populous Indian country before reaching south to join the Ohio. Due south of Fort Wayne was the fort-studded road to Fort Washington and Cincinnati at the mouth of the Miami.

In late October 1794 General Wayne returned to Greenville. The Legion, those not garrisoning Fort Wayne and Fort Defiance, went into winter quarters. General Scott took his Kentuckians home. General Anthony Wayne had won his war and defeated his enemy. All that remained for him to do was to take the submission of his enemies and arrive at a just peace. The first was accomplished by President Washington's birthday in 1795. To achieve the second Wayne called a council of the chiefs to be held at Greenville in the spring.

By mid-June eleven hundred Indians with their women and children had pitched their camps at Greenville. On 16 June the chief men of twelve Indian nations sat down with General Wayne to work out some way for people to live together in the American Northwest. The dignity of the Indian matched the discipline of the Legion as both sides met in amity and good will. Markedly absent, physically and in influence, were the British. By Jay's Treaty they had given up their claim to American land, and by their unfulfilled promises to the Indians they had lost the friendship of the Indian nations. After six weeks of oratory and formality and felicity the council was agreed. Boundaries were set around twenty-five thousand square miles and sixteen fort enclaves which would be wholly owned by the United States. A cash settlement of $20,000 and an annuity of $9,500 were given in consideration thereof. The remaining land belonged to the nations according to their homelands. In addition to the territorial apportionment it was understood that the red man would benefit by learning the white man's good ways of tilling the soil and his methods of industry. All would profit and be content in a lasting peace.

The treaty was read twice to the assemblage, ringed around by all the Indian watchers and off-duty soldiers. General Wayne rose from his chair and, turning first to the Chippewa delegation, asked if they would sign the document as read. Solemnly, the Chippewa chiefs gave their assent. Then the chiefs of each nation in turn, Ottawa, Potawatomi, Wyandot, Delaware, Shawnee, Miami, Wea, Kickapoo, Piankeshaw, Kaskaskia, Eel River, were asked, and they all gave their assent. Two or three days would be needed to inscribe the treaty on parchment and to make twelve fair copies. Wayne adjourned the council until 2 August and, while they waited for the ceremony of signing, invited all present to a feast. By the tenth of the month all the Indians had gone to their homes, and in Greenville the Legion of the United States went back to soldiering.

Little Turtle went home to a new house, built for him by soldiers of the Legion of the United States.

Whatever lay in the past, in the tall Miami chief, whose skin was lighter than that of many black Irishmen making Pennsylvania whisky, General Wayne recognized wisdom and leadership. Little Turtle had been the first of the Indians to see the weakness of the British and the strength of the United States in the year 1795 and for the decade ahead. As the Miami had been first to war under Little Turtle in 1790, under the same leader they were first to peace in 1795. And under that wise leadership the other nations came to the council of Greenville to make peace. The United States Government was appreciative and built the chief (who signed his name "Meshekunnoghguoh" at Greenville) a fine house near Fort Wayne. Little Turtle, his wars over at the age of forty-eight, accepted the gift of his former enemy and devoted the remainder of his life to keeping the peace that he, above all Indians, had helped to bring about.

The itinerant, warring Shawnee had been the most reluctant of the twelve nations who attended the council. Their great chief, Blue Jacket, had challenged the leadership of Little Turtle before Fallen Timbers, and he had forced the Miami to set the ambush. Blue Jacket's Shawnee had been the last of the nations to arrive at Greenville. Tecumseh, the brilliant young war chief and Blue Jacket's protégé, had not come at all.

At twenty-seven, Tecumseh found himself in an unfamiliar and unwanted time of peace. The war of a lifetime left him homeless, his father, three brothers, his foster father, and scores of his friends had been killed by the Americans. He had a brother who was contaminated by the white man's whisky. A sister lived in Chillocothe, on the Mad River. Old Piqua, the home of Tecumseh's youth, had been destroyed and the new

Piqua was not home to him. In his search for a new place Tecumseh married a half-breed woman who bore him a son. They could not hold him.

For a time Tecumseh did find peace in a strange place. A pioneer farmer in Ohio opened his home to the young Indian, and his daughter, Rebecca, made Tecumseh welcome in it. The fair blonde girl taught him to read and speak English. By candlelight they studied the words and meaning of the Bible. As he progressed, Tecumseh read of the lives of great leaders who had won wars and made nations. The felicity of the Galloway home ended abruptly when the call of Tecumseh's Indian blood became a shout of warning. He left the hospitable Galloways, taking with him the treasure of an education and the memory of the blonde girl that he might have married.

From Ohio, Tecumseh removed to Indiana. Although Indiana lay outside the treaty land, which included the lands later to be called Illinois, it was declared a territory of the United States in 1800, and William Henry Harrison was appointed its first governor. With his new-found voice of indignation, Tecumseh protested. With a loud shout, he marked each new incursion into the Indian lands. He spoke out to any Indian of any nation who would listen. His anger turned on the Indian chiefs, who, by individual treaties, had ceded Indian land to the Americans. Tecumseh's premise was that all Indian lands belonged mutually to all Indians and no chief could sell them or give them away without the consent of all Indians. Many of the young men listened to Tecumseh's idea of Indian unity. The old chiefs, with their reason and their pensions, shook their heads. They remembered Pontiac who, in their youth, would have made one nation of all Indians. But wisdom and experience could not damp the fresh new wind rustling through the dried cornstalks and shaking the established ridgepoles of the winter lodges. Like drifting leaves in autumn, young warriors gathered in the shelter of the windbreak called up by Tecumseh's pride in being an Indian.

Lalawethika, Tecumseh's drunken brother, raised the tempo of the wind to a gale, and, with his religious fanaticism, he created a storm. As the white man with his strong drink had shown Lalawethika the depths of depravity, so the white man's religion lifted him to the pinnacle of ecstasy. The religious revivalists who spread through the Northwest in 1805 included the sect of Shakers. Somehow their quaking trancelike dancing penetrated the fog of alcohol eating at the drunken Indian's brain. A severe illness with a high fever sobered Lalawethika long enough to permit him to remember that in his delirium he had met and talked with the Indian Master of Life. He became a reformed man, and with the zeal of the reformed, Lalawethika preached the evil of drink. The hallucinations that had come with his illness continued, and the Master of Life continued to guide his dramatic utterances. He changed his name, taking the words of Christ "I am the door," which in the Shawnee tongue was "Tenskwatawa." Indians were drawn to the Shawnee Prophet as inevitably they were drawn to any odd person among them. They heeded the strange man, blind in one eye, who wore a drooping line of black hair across his upper lip, in the white man's way, as they listened to his handsome brother. The quivering Tenskwatawa talked with God and stirred their awe and wonder. The upstanding Tecumseh talked to them of hope and offered leadership. Tecumseh took charge of his mystical brother and shrewdly combined their preaching. The Master of Life, too, ceased his invective against drink and through his Prophet more and more frequently sent a message of hate of the white man and a command to return to the ways of the Indian.

Together, the brothers built a great lodge near Greenville, the place of the Indians' shame, and there their followers gathered. Another center for teaching grew up near Vincennes, the old French city that Governor Harrison had made his capital.

The legend of the Prophet, as the white men called Tenskwatawa, grew. It was said that, challenged by the governor to perform a miracle, the Prophet darkened the sun at midday. The Indians believed this tale, though the white men said that the English had forewarned Tecumseh of an eclipse. The story spread that Tecumseh and Tenskwatawa were twins, always a source of wonder among Indians. This was increased to triplets, even more wonderful. The third brother was said to be living elsewhere or to have been killed in battle with the white man. All this enhanced the influence of the brothers. Tecumseh denied nothing.

The times being quiet for the moment, Tecumseh set off on the evangelist's trail, and took his unstable brother with him. They spoke in all the villages in the Northwest. Tenskwatawa quivered, looked horrible, and sonorously prophesied disaster. Tecumseh, with the rich oratory that he had mastered, invited the councils to join him in Indian unity. By becoming a single heart, a single body politic, a single voice, a single arm of force, the Indian nations could save themselves and their lands. American expansion would be forced to halt at the wall of united Indian determination. War would be too big, too terrible for the Americans if the nations that had signed the Greenville council, and others west and south, would unite and face the United States of America as a single nation of equal strength.

Most of the young warriors espoused the cause of unity and looked to Tecumseh for leadership. Many moved their homes to the Prophet's Town on the Tippecanoe. By 1810 there were a thousand fighting men there: not enough to fight, not enough to bargain with, but enough to show a growing strength. In 1809 Tecumseh had met in council with the Seminole in Florida and other Indians on the Americans' southern flank. In the same year he had gone among the powerful Osage in the west, beyond the Mississippi. With many distant nations he made alliance. But the old chiefs of the Northwest refused to heed the call for Indian unity. They and their followers stayed on the treaty land and inched into white civilization like a green worm creeping along the stick of time.

IX

The Governor of Indiana

At twenty-one William Henry Harrison was a proven soldier at war, faced with the duty of keeping the peace. General Wayne had cited his young aide by name in the dispatches that had been sent to Washington, telling of the victory at Fallen Timbers. For a lieutenant, mention in dispatches was a public attestation to his courage and a private recommendation for advancement in his profession. For the victor there is the triumph, and at twenty-one triumph is sweet, and humility, though becoming, is a difficult posture to assume. In the uniform of the Legion, his flat cocked hat jauntily askew on his head, Lieutenant Harrison walked through the congress of Greenville on errands for his general. In 1796 General Wayne made his tour of the new lands released by the British under the terms of Jay's Treaty. At Detroit, in the final gesture of triumph, he saw the starred and stripped flag go up over the citadel and the way to the upper lakes open to the United States. Shortly thereafter, on the American shore of Lake Erie, "Mad Anthony Wayne" died and was buried in sorrow by his men.

William Henry Harrison returned to his regimental duties and in May of 1797 he was promoted to captain in the 1st Regiment of Infantry. The Legion of the United States had disappeared six months before Harrison's promotion, to be continued as attenuated regiments of the U.S. army—infantry, artillery, and two companies of light dragoons, culled from the old sub-legions. That Harrison survived the combing out of officers spoke well for his future. That he was given command of Fort Washington proved the high regard in which he was held.

The site of Fort Washington should have been at North Bend on the Ohio, but the ensign charged with building the fort was paying attention at the time to the wife of a settler who lived at a place called Cincinnati, on the river opposite the Licking River. The original blockhouse there was expanded to a fort, but what the punitive expeditions needed was a base downriver from Pittsburgh. The flatboats of the early settlers had drifted past the log walls of Fort Washington, usually stopping for information as to the chance of ambush below, and for a night of rest under protection of the soldiers. After the peace at Greenville the expanded fort and the village growing up around it saw a torrent of settlers, who passed by with only a wave of the arm and a friendly shout.

The year 1795 was the year of a second great migration into the western lands. Britain and Spain, occupied with European affairs, no longer menaced the perimeter of the United States. A genuine Indian peace made the interior secure for the farmer, the merchant, and the developer. The independent settlers and the adventurers, once isolated, were being joined by a crowd of less hardy immigrants from beyond the

Alleghenies. All who lived west of the mountains were grateful to the army that curbed the Indian raids, and the judges and officials, appointed or elected, held the respect of the westerners. George Washington's dream of a greater United States had become a reality. His trans-mountain canal was never built, but the old trails were expanded into good wagon roads that carried families to the west and a growing volume of commerce to the east. By 1800 Kentucky was a state with two hundred and twenty thousand inhabitants. Tennessee achieved its requisite seventy-five thousand population in 1796 and continued to grow as a state. New Englanders moved across New York State and into the Western Reserve of Connecticut that lay along the south shore of Lake Erie and that, in 1800, was a part of the new Ohio Territory. From Pittsburgh, at the end of old first roads over the mountains, settlers moved north into Ohio and met their fellow Ohioans in the Western Reserve. Only those bound for western Kentucky and the further Northwest passed by Fort Washington, but to the veteran soldiers, watching for the arrival of their new commanding officer, their numbers were impressive.

Life was static in the confines of the rambling log stockade, set in fifteen acres of preserve, and particularly so for a twenty-four-year-old captain. The housekeeping and school-teaching of peacetime soldiering was dull. There was no place to go, no place to lead his troops but up, down, and around the barracks square. There was no encouragement from the government in Philadelphia, which had forgotten the army except as a department whose expenses could be pared. Brigadier General Wilkinson, who had succeeded to the command of the army, was neither the man nor the leader that Anthony

Wayne had been. Nor could Harrison, a former aide of General Wayne, expect favor from the man whom the hero of Stony Point and Fallen Timbers had held in contempt and suspicion. From the covered watchtower of Fort Washington, Captain Harrison, with much idle time, watched the flatboats gliding westward with the current.

The area around Fort Washington was the Virginian captain's home in the west. In 1795 William Henry Harrison had married Anna Symmes, who lived at North Bend, Indiana. There the couple made their home. Harrison's father-in-law had been a judge in New Jersey, and on going to the Northwest he had been appointed United States district judge. As such, he was the Law throughout the long stretch of the Ohio River. Like all men in the west, except for the idle and forgotten soldiers waiting out their duty, Judge Symmes was busy planning and developing the new country. His most immediate project was the transformation of the village next to Fort Washington into the city of Cincinnati. For a year, Captain Harrison watched the life going on around his quiet fort. Then on 1 June 1798 he resigned his commission and stepped out through the wide gate to join the busy world. Soon after his retirement the post of Secretary of the Northwest became vacant, and William Henry Harrison was appointed to fill the vacancy.

Opportunity and advancement came fast to the young westerner. In 1799, Harrison was sent by the Jeffersonian party to Congress as delegate from the Northwest Territory. Active, personable, and well-connected in the east as well as in the west, Harrison was in the right place at the right time. In January 1800 he was designated Governor of Indiana, the new territory that included all the Old Northwest except Ohio, which was soon to become a state.

Harrison was not sworn into his new office until January 1801, when he returned to the west and made his home and his capital in the old French town of Vincennes, on the Wabash River. On the three hundred acres that he purchased, the governor had a fine mansion built for him. *Grouseland* was a fitting place for his official dignity and for Anna and the children. The house, nevertheless, was partly a fort—an imposing residence in which to receive and impress the Indian chiefs who came to see the governor.

William Henry Harrison's first duty was to the citizens of the United States, who were migrating into the Indian lands, as the name "Indiana" implied. While at the national capital he had devised a scheme to put the public land of his territory into the hands of the settlers at terms favorable to them. Upon taking office, he worked hard on that scheme, but he soon realized that in order to satisfy the demand, he must acquire more land to sell. More land could only be had by treaty purchase from the Indian nations living by right in Indiana. The first such treaty was made at Fort Wayne. It was Harrison's first treaty, too, and he came to the negotiations not only as governor, but also as a special commissioner. Other councils and treaties followed: Vincennes in 1804 and *Grouseland* in 1805. As a result of these councils, Governor Harrison gained more public lands in southern Indiana, Illinois, Wisconsin, and Missouri on which to settle white immigrants.

Sometimes the extent of the governor's responsibilities was beyond the physical power even of a strong and active young man such as William Henry Harrison. For a few short months his domain even included all of the Louisiana Purchase, which President Jefferson had bought in 1803. But that added responsibility was only temporary; other arrangements were soon made there. Even the Indiana Territory, in the Old Northwest, was divided into future state entities. In 1805 the map-makers in the eastern seat of government sliced the Michigan peninsula off from Indiana and gave it to old William Hull to govern as a new territory. While in Philadelphia William Henry Harrison had been one of the makers of the new political map of the west. He therefore watched with equanimity while Illinois was made a territory and his own Indiana circumscribed, east, north, south, and west. By 1809, when the Wabash River had become Indiana's western limit, the aims of the territorial governor were increased population and statehood. In the first decade of the nineteenth century, twenty thousand immigrants had come into Indiana. They had settled in the south where the public lands were for sale. The Indians owned the northern part and much of the middle of the territory. If Indiana were to meet its population requirement for statehood, then the governor had to acquire more public land to offer as inducement to new homesteaders. Harrison could get more land only from the Indians. So, in 1809, William Henry Harrison called the Indians to a council, to be held at Fort Wayne. Little Turtle came from his house near by and was received with veneration by the Indians of three of the Greenville nations and by the young governor against whom he had fought. The council agreed that, for $8,200 and an annuity of $2,350, three million acres on the Wabash and White rivers would pass into the public domain of the United States. Two others of the

Greenville nations, who were not represented at the council of
Fort Wayne, later subscribed to the treaty.

In every possible way, Governor Harrison protected the
Indians who shared his territory. They were under his
protection and they were his responsibility. He gave them
respect and fair value. At the request of the chiefs, he did what
he could to keep from the Indians the strong drink that
physically and mentally demoralized them. Although William
Henry Harrison lived in concord with the chiefs of the treaty
nations, a renegade band under Tecumseh and the Prophet
were against him.

As early as 1808, Governor Harrison had denounced the
two brothers to the Shawnee nation. The new Prophet's
Town on the Tippecanoe had become a menace and a danger
to the peace of Indiana. Before going to the council at Fort
Wayne, Governor Harrison had called the Shawnee Prophet
(Tecumseh was away) to Vincennes. The governor, in neat
military dress, confronted the misshapen holy man, and
accused him to his face of conniving with the British to the
north. Tenskwatawa denied the charge, and shrilled a renewal
of his vow of friendship for the United States of America.

Trouble flared up again when Tecumseh returned from his
travels and learned of the transaction that had been made at
Fort Wayne. He contended that the Indian nations at the
council did not own the land they had sold to the Americans.
He reiterated that all the land belonged to all Indians
communally. Tecumseh's anger was not directed solely against
the chiefs; to him they were only pitiful old men, stumbling
slaves after the white man, defilers of the old ways in council,
and enemies of the new way of Indian unity. In faultless

rhetoric he flayed Governor Harrison with abuse, calling the
governor a lackey of bad faith, a chanter of false promises, a
purveyor of liquor that muddled the brains of the doddering
council. Tenskwatawa said seven amens to the last charge.
The young warriors of the new way danced for war. But
Tecumseh was not yet ready to end the peace.

The long winter in the lodges was a time to nurture hate. In
the spring of 1810 the boat came from Vincennes as usual,
bringing the annuity to Prophet's Town. Tecumseh's Indians
crowded the shore, threatening the boatmen and calling them
"American dogs." The annuity was refused and the boat was
followed downstream by the yelping of the Indian villagers.
On two later occasions Governor Harrison sent messengers to
the Prophet's Town, but the Frenchmen he sent were turned
back as spies. Finally, Tecumseh was able to persuade his
brother and his followers to receive the third scout who came
to Tippecanoe. Tecumseh accepted Harrison's invitation to a
conference, and noted that the invitation was to him alone and
that he was to bring not more than thirty warriors as escort.

On the morning of 12 August Tecumseh appeared at
Vincennes. With him were four hundred warriors, all omi-
nously dressed and armed. The people of Vincennes saw that
the Indian camp was a bivouac. There were few Indian
women with their men. Their camp was that of a war party,
not a family gathering for the feasting and barter of a peaceful
council.

When the time came for Harrison and Tecumseh to meet
and talk, they did so with their respective followers tense and
watchful all around them. For a long moment anger leapt
between the two men and the peace of fifteen years trembled.

But Tecumseh had other journeys to make, more allies to rally, more warriors to recruit, before he could make his war. William Henry Harrison was more ready to make a fight for peace than was his Indian rival, but not with four hundred armed Indians in his capital.

The council between the two young leaders ended in polite respect, underscored by a recognized rivalry to the death. Then the Indian leader left Vincennes for far-ranging travels that would take him finally into the welcoming arms of the British on the Great Lakes.

The American governor stayed at his home, *Grouseland*. He had decided that in the next year he would lead a punitive expedition to the Prophet's Town, either to neutralize its menace or to destroy it. William Henry Harrison had been taught by "Mad Anthony Wayne" to attack, but the general had also trained his aide to plan and prepare. Governor Harrison reached for his quill and called for his secretary. He would need a Regiment of Infantry. The 4th would be available to him. John Parke Boyd was its colonel. He had until recently been in the Army of the Nizam of Hyderabad in India. Governor Scott of Kentucky was the General Scott who had fought at Fallen Timbers, and Harrison could count on him for a good contingent of riflemen. James Wilkinson commanded the U.S. army. William Eustis of Boston was Secretary of War and Indian Affairs. Above all these was President James Madison. All would have to concur with Governor Harrison's plans, and they all did. The plans for the expedition went forward through the winter of 1810–11.

X

Tippecanoe

In the spring of 1811 the federal government in its new capital of Washington City gave Governor Harrison discretionary powers within his territory. By midsummer, enthusiastic Indiana militiamen had rallied in Vincennes to go against the Prophet's Town, to sweep it away like a wasps' nest in the rafters of a barn. Harrison waited on two events before starting his expedition: the departure of Tecumseh on a long journey to the Indian nations of the south, and the arrival at his own capital of the regular soldiers.

The 4th Regiment, U.S. Infantry, which Governor Harrison welcomed with the appraising eye of a former soldier, was pitifully under strength. Even for an army neglected by politicians, less than three hundred officers and men in an establishment calling for some eight hundred was scandalously few. Yet these men, of indifferent presence and as yet uninitiated in battle, had the bearing of discipline and the aura of continuity so lacking in the ad hoc militia of independent air. Most of the militia were Indiana men, intent on revenge. Kentucky, remembering old wrongs, sent a small contingent of mounted men heavy with good officers. Two of these, Kentucky General Samuel Wells and Colonel Joseph Hamilton Daviess, who was a lawyer, took command of the two hundred cavalry, divided into dragoons and mounted rifles. The four hundred remaining militiamen were the infantry in support of Colonel Boyd's three hundred regulars.

The nine hundred men left Vincennes on 26 September. They marched along the riverbank, keeping company with the supply boats. John Tipton, mounted on his good mare, appraised the bottomland as rich, and marveled at the prairie that they crossed. He was one of those who found a bee tree and, with his friend George Spencer, smoked it out and distributed the honey among the company. About sixty miles above Vincennes, two miles north of an abandoned Wea village, Harrison called a halt.

There, in the now classic method of penetrating Indian country, Harrison built a fort. The soldiers worked through October setting the stakes and building the three-cornered blockhouses. Tipton was busy. He was a blacksmith and a gunsmith, and he was a gambler. He shot at the mark in practice, for money, whisky, for leggings, for whatever else he needed. When five Delaware Indians came in friendship to the camp, John Tipton was pleased to find that their leader played at cards.

At last the fort was finished, and Colonel/Lawyer Daviess, a bottle of whisky in his hand, made an eloquent speech in dedication of Fort Harrison. As he smashed the bottle against the gatepost, the soldiers groaned. Additional supplies arrived on the 28 October, the day of the dedication, escorted by reinforcements of mounted men from Kentucky. Harrison was ready to move on to the Prophet's Town.

They marched upriver, crossing to the west bank where the prairie, some of it burned over, stretched all the way to Fort Dearborn at Chicago on Lake Michigan. As the course of the Wabash bore to the west the land changed to flat forestland with scattered old Indian cornfields. On 2 November, General Harrison built a blockhouse as a staging stop for river traffic. He continued the march fully operational. The packs of the infantry were now carried in the wagons. The cavalry rode point and flank guard. The foot soldiers marched in a broken column a mile long, ready to change flank and direction quickly on attack. Early on 6 November the point reported seeing Indians. More and more Indians were seen as the morning wore on. The army was now marching on either side of the wide road that led directly to the Prophet's Town. Only a mile and a half ahead, a delegation of chiefs was waiting in the road to receive Governor Harrison and offer him a parley with Tenskwatawa the next day. They volunteered to show the governor a good place to camp the night. Two officers, sent to view the campsite reported it excellent. Warily, but keeping the good faith of diplomacy with skepticism, General Harrison moved the army onto the designated campground, and set alert guards.

The army slept well. A Negro camp follower who had been missing was found prowling around the general's tent. He was marched away under close arrest. None of the watchful sentries, however, noticed that Harrison's white horse had pulled its tether. On the northwest corner of the camp, Stephen Mars stood the last watch of the night. He was a

Kentucky man, and he kept a good watch from the high bank above the scrub and the high grasses of the wet prairie along the creek. The night grew even colder just before dawn.

In the Indian town they neither watched nor slept. The moon of vision was in the Prophet that night, and again and again he told of victory in the morning. With Tecumseh away, there was no one to stay him. The Prophet brought out the magic beans that would turn the white man's bullets to drops of water and the long knives to twigs. Armed with the wonderful magic, the warriors set out for the camp of the Americans. Sometime after three o'clock in the morning, the Prophet took up his stand a safe distance from Harrison's outposts, while the warriors crawled forward to encircle the sleeping soldiers.

General Harrison was sitting on his camp bed, pulling on his boots in preparation for the pre-dawn stand-to, when Stephen Mars sensed a movement in the prairie grass below the bank where he watched. All around the lone sentry there was an unseen stirring. He fired at the first shadow he saw move, and shouting loudly, turned to run back into the camp.

Harrison heard the shot, and the fusillade of shots that followed. The long war whoops came quickly after; then the yells of startled men, jerked suddenly from their deep sleep. The governor shouted for his strayed horse, as the steady voices of the officers rose above the tumult.

At the northwest corner of the camp, where Stephen Mars now lay dead, Captain Robert Barton of the 4th Infantry commanded a company. The soldiers there were fighting hand to hand. Mounted at last on a strong bay, Governor Harrison was soon at the broken angle with a reserve company coming on. Now the point of danger shifted to the northeast corner of the camp, where a large band of frenzied Indians, feeling themselves secure in their promised immortality, were attacking. Harrison was there, the bay caracoling under the unfamiliar hands. He put Colonel Daviess's mounted men into a counterattack. Dashing into the dark before his attack was fully mounted, the eloquent Kentuckian was thrown from his horse, himself with a mortal wound. Captain Josiah Snelling and a company of the 4th wheeled out of line, completed the attack begun by Daviess, and returned to their place. Some of the bayonets were wet with blood.

All through the last minutes of darkness, Harrison rode to the wildest sound of firing. Behind the perimeter lines, reserve companies jogged through the tents, wagons and horse lines to the threatened points. All held firm while they waited for the dawn.

The first light came slowly into the oak wood, showing the faces of the men as they took aim at the dim figures moving behind the bushes. The growing light showed clearly the dark forms of the dead. With the coming of day, Governor Harrison saw the Indians massed on his flanks. Before he could order an attack, Major Samuel Wells charged north with the infantry. The Indians gave ground. On the south flank, too, the Indians were driven back by regulars, riflemen, and militiamen, all charging together. The Indians took refuge in the wet lands, where the cavalry could not follow, and with astonishment examined their wounds.

On his safe hillock the Prophet sat, shouting incantations and conjuring profound spells. More and more Indians came up to him to show their wounds and tell of the many dead.

The Prophet first sought to exhort them, then to fabricate excuses. As the Indians gathered around him their disenchantment grew, and they left him there, frantically making magic, until, terrified, he, too, got up and fled.

The day after the battle, William Henry Harrison set his soldiers to burning down the Prophet's Town. The place was empty. Gone were the Indians, back to the villages of the Chippewa, the Miami, the Kickapoo, the Ottawa, the Potawatomi, the Sac and Fox, the Shawnee, the Winnebego, and the Wyandot. The lodgepole of Tecumseh's empire of all Indians, cast down in the battle of Tippecanoe, was consumed in the fire of the Prophet's Town.

The victorious army returned to the downriver settlements. Cheers and fêtes followed each contingent on its triumphal way, each man to his ultimate welcome home. They had fought well for General Harrison in the oak wood that November morning, taking their casualties, one hundred and eighty-eight killed and wounded, as steadily in attack as under attack. The soldiers, militiamen and regulars, were heroes and saviors to all the west, and all western men were lifted up by the great victory at Tippecanoe. The battle fought on 7 November 1811 made every dream seem possible to the nation-builders beyond the Alleghenies. The British, whom no American held blameless for any Indian rising, could be driven from their forts north of the lake. All of Upper Canada, to its unknown west and north, could be incorporated into the fast-growing American west.

While the blooded veterans of the 4th Infantry were still settling into winter quarters at Fort Harrison, the congressmen from the western states were riding down the Atlantic slopes of the Alleghenies. As they rode together, they talked of war with England and the annexation of the farther side of the upper lakes. Along the roads and at the overnight inns of Virginia, the western congressmen began to meet their colleagues from further south, where Spain still held continental land. As they converged on Washington City they plotted their strategy for the twelfth Congress of the United States of America. They were all of an opinion that the tangled issues of the last decade must finally be resolved in a war with England.

XI

Isaac Brock of Upper Canada

Tecumseh was still fighting when, in early June 1812, he crossed the Detroit River to the British side and presented himself at the gate of Fort Amherst. He had returned from his embassy to the total disaster of the Prophet's Town. His brother was gone, useless to him now, a wanderer displaying conjurer's tricks of magic in which no one believed. The loyal warriors were gone from the Prophet's Town, disillusioned by their Prophet but perhaps not totally lost to their leader, Tecumseh, in the fight against the Americans. The winter was long for Tecumseh and the few close followers who sat with him in a lonely forest lodge. In the spring Tecumseh offered himself, his loyalty, his influence, and his followers to the British.

Colonel Matthew Elliott, British Agent of the Indian Department, welcomed the proud man, Tecumseh—The Shooting Star. It was Elliott's office which had launched Tecumseh on his meteoric course across the Indian sky. After Greenville, the Indian Department had gone against official

British policy by giving guns and supplies to the dissident Shawnee and the thirty who then followed him. In backing Tecumseh, the agent had adjured him against making premature war against the long knives of the Americans. The Shooting Star had followed that policy, proven right by the disaster which befell the false Prophet at Tippecanoe. But as Tecumseh and Elliott met again at Fort Malden, war was maturing between Britain and the United States, and a new policy was in the process of formation.

Colonel Elliott had as much need for the Indian leader as Tecumseh had for him. At the furthermost end of the empire, Upper Canada, which included Fort Malden, was all but forsaken by the mother government in London. Since the demonstrations in France had turned to riots, to the slaughter of the Revolution, Britain's king and parliament had been fully occupied with European affairs. The chaotic failure of the French Revolution had led logically to the opportunism of Napoleon and to the achievement of his ambition for a military dictatorship. England's opposition to the Corsican "ogre" involved every branch of His Majesty's government in the battle for empire. England was fighting with laws in parliament, hard diplomacy, trade and commerce and industry, with a thousand warships at sea, and finally, with her small army, attacking out of Portugal. Between 1805 and 1812 the British government had little energy and no soldiers to spend in the wild woods of Upper Canada where Bonaparte was not a threat.

As caretakers of Canada, England relied on the character, courage, ability, and wisdom of the few men in authority there. She was well served in Upper Canada by Isaac Brock.

Routine and rotation had brought Brock to Canada. A subaltern by purchase at the age of sixteen, the young Guernsey boy had risen rapidly to lieutenant colonel at twenty-eight in 1797. Colonel Brock had fought his regiment in the Low Countries against French revolutionaries and as marines aboard Nelson's ships at Copenhagen. In 1802 Brock, with his 41st Regiment, was posted to Canada, far away from the action and the glory and the chance of quick promotion when the French Wars had become the Napoleonic Wars. As he moved up and down the lakes and rivers, Isaac Brock studied and planned the defense of Canada against the brash Yankees to the south. He received the authority to implement many of his ideas in 1810, on his promotion to "Major General on the Staff of North America." Civil responsibilities became the duty of most senior British officers serving in the colonies, and to General Brock was given the post of president and administrator of Upper Canada.

The seat of government in Upper Canada was at York, on the north shore of Lake Ontario. The site for the town had been selected for strategic reasons. York stood between Kingston, at the head of the St. Lawrence, and the Niagara River settlements, so vulnerable to sudden attack by the Americans on the south banks of both rivers. Through the capital passed strategic roads, Yonge, Danforth, and Dundas streets, connecting Lower Canada with Upper Canada, both north and west to Niagara and beyond, to the border with Michigan along the Detroit River. The lakes themselves were strategic highways, guarded on the Canadian side by forts opposing other forts on the American side of the interflow of each lake. Thus Fort Malden confronted Detroit upriver, and the little British post on St. Joseph Island guarded the portage to Lake Superior, while Michimilinac paired with it to watch the entrance to America's Lake Michigan. At the far end of Lake Superior, the Northwest Company's Fort William stood alone, marking the beginning of the scarcely imagined Canadian west and north.

General Brock, newly established in his capital at York, was aware of both the strategic strength and weakness of his province when spring came on in 1812. He knew that in April the American militia had been called out and that open war could be expected. To meet that threat he had but few regulars, the possibility of Indian help, and the militia, which he had been honing into a defense force of problematic keenness.

In all Canada there were only some four hundred thousand souls, mostly of French extraction. The population of Upper Canada, though English-speaking, were immigrants from the old colonies on the Atlantic seaboard. Of these, many were Loyalist refugee Tories who, by 1812, had added to their numbers a second generation of militia-age men. These young men were staunch Canadians. Of doubtful loyalty were the new immigrants from the United States. These people were of the same stock as the belligerent anti-English Kentuckians, Ohioans, and Northwesterners. In all, Brock had eleven thousand men of militia age in Upper Canada, including both empire Loyalists and new Canadians. He pared this number down to four thousand reliable militiamen, all volunteers, whom he favored with the best arms and with the title of flank companies within the mass of the militia organization.

In his plan for the defense of Upper Canada, General Brock,

knowing the bad repair of the streets, had to rely on the waterways for transport and quick movement. This required a lake navy. As early as 1808 the Americans had put a 16-gun brig on Lake Ontario, and two officers of the U.S. navy (one of them a boy midshipman named James Fenimore Cooper) had surreptitiously mapped Kingston Harbor. When the Royal Navy had shown no inclination to put fleets on the Great Lakes, the Canadian militia had found sailors for a Provincial Marine.

By the spring of 1812 the militia navy had a frigate on Lake Ontario, and in mid-June *Hunter,* fully manned and gunned, rode at anchor off Fort Malden. The flank companies all over the province were turning out for training, exercise, and instruction at least six days in a month. Robert Dickson, the fur trader, reported to Isaac Brock that two hundred and fifty to three hundred Indians were available as auxiliaries. The word from Detroit that Tecumseh had taken the oath to the Crown increased the prospect for a much more active guerrilla warfare being carried into the western territories. Under arms, General Brock had the 41st Regiment on the establishment of the British army, a few gunners of the Royal Artillery, and the potential of new, quasi-regular, fencible regiments. Brock's defense force in Upper Canada was a well-planned, potentially adequate array. But with only fifteen hundred men under arms at the end of the first fortnight of June 1812, and a thousand-mile border to protect, General Brock was vulnerable on the ground. Nevertheless he was better prepared for war than were the bellicose Yankees south of the lakes and rivers.

XII

Free Trade and Sailors' Rights

During Isaac Brock's decade of planning a military defense of Canada, the government of the United States, with idealistic ferocity, had been waging peace against both France and England, the prime belligerents of Europe at war. Thomas Jefferson, always a man of peace and reason, believed in an army of ministers armed with embargoes, aimed at the enemies' economy. The Napoleonic Wars had an economic phase that had begun in 1806 with the French Dictator's "Decrees," which raised a paper blockade around the British Isles. George III had retaliated by promulgating the "Orders in Council," which forbade the neutral nations from trading with Continental Europe. The king's move was effective, as he had the ships and sailors to enforce his blockade. The Orders in Council and the Decrees fell heaviest on the United States, which was the last neutral with a significant carrying trade on the seas. Jefferson, a staunch advocate of free trade, found in the double blockade an opportunity to test in practice his theory of bloodless war by economic boycott. Although his

ministers in London and Paris protested and lodged com-
plaints, Jefferson steered his Embargo Act through his docile
Congress.

The Act was a two-edged weapon of non-violence, forged
to cut at both France and England. By forbidding American
ships to take cargo and sail from American ports, the Embargo
Act denied matériel and substance to both belligerents. In
theory, too, the embargo kept American ships and sailors from
inciting incidents which might embroil the United States in a
shooting war. But Mr. Jefferson's law was a weapon that
proved to be sharper on the backstroke than against the enemy.
The industrial and commercial men of New England, Federalists opposed to the Jeffersonian Republicans, yelped as the
sword fell on their means of livelihood.

A precocious thirteen-year-old poet, studying Latin, flailed
the Embargo Act as "terrapin policy," and likened it to a
sweeping wind where "fear lowers before and famine stalks
behind." The New England merchants, less poetic than
William Cullen Bryant, disregarded the paper embargo and
found smuggling to be practical, profitable, and easy. The
British blockade ships let the laden Yankee merchantmen out
of the American ports and saw them safely in to Britain or to
Portugal, where a hungry British army waited their coming.
As France could not get American trade because of the British
blockade of Europe, the New England Federalists claimed that
by excluding trade with Britain the Embargo Act favored
Napoleon, whom they detested. The boy poet fixed the
Embargo Act on his little rapier as "French intrigue, which
wheedles to devour." On the eve of the election of 1808
Thomas Jefferson, Republican party leader as well as Presi-

dent, was hard pressed on his Northeastern money flank. Before a mortal political blow could strike down his party, President Jefferson backed off from his futile economic war. The Republicans elected their candidate, James Madison, William Cullen Bryant went back to his academic studies, and "free trade" remained a slogan for Americans to shout.

"Sailors' Rights" was the other phrase of the slogan that war-minded people chanted during the first years of little Mr. Madison's presidency. "Free Trade and Sailors' Rights" was the banner under which the frigates of the U.S. navy sailed out to make war in June of 1812. For too long, too many American men had been pressed into the man-hungry British navy by boarding parties, strong and arrogant under the big guns of a broadside battery. The British officer would claim any well set-up Yankee as a British subject or a deserter and hustle the man off to servitude aboard His Majesty's ship. Nor did the boarding parties prey only on the merchant ships.

On 22 June 1807 *H.M.S. Leopard* stopped the outbound *U.S.S. Chesapeake* in international waters off Norfolk, claiming three deserters were aboard. The men in question were the pressed men William Ware and John Strachan, both of Maryland's eastern shore, and Ware's shipmate, Daniel Martin, a freed man from Massachusetts. All three had escaped from a British 38-gun ship blockading Chesapeake Bay. Commodore James Barron refused to give up the three American sailors aboard his ship. The boarding party left. *Leopard* opened fire, and *Chesapeake,* guns all secured for sea, could only get one gun in action before Commodore Barron, with three dead and his rigging a shambles, struck the colors. The British boarding party returned aboard *Chesapeake,* found the three and a fourth man who was a true deserter, and took them away to a flogging on the grating and the unremitting work of the foredeck.

When *Chesapeake* returned to Norfolk with her dead and wounded, her damage and her humbled pride, the whole American seaboard was ready to begin the War of 1812. Only the calm reason and political strength of Jefferson kept America from war that summer of 1807. As the temper of the nation cooled, James Madison, the Secretary of State, began diplomatic negotiations for the return of the three sailors.

James Madison was President when, five years later, the *Leopard* affair was successfully concluded by the United States. Patience had triumphed in the cause of peace. Patience, too, had served Martin and Strachan and Ware through five years of servitude. All three lived through their ordeal to return to a homeland where patience had run out.

"Free Trade and Sailors' Rights" had become a meaningful slogan when Ware and Martin and Strachan at long last set foot on the American shore. "Free Trade and Sailors' Rights" was the banner in the beaks of the "War Hawks" who had swept in from the west to seize the new capital building in Washington City. Where Thomas Jefferson had held his party and his Congress to his pacific principles, his successor, Mr. Madison, with his formidable wife at home in the President's palace, was no match for the War Hawk congressmen who represented the landed citizens of the west and south. The War Hawks wanted the wide lands of Canada, which to their minds was a lost fourteenth colony, rightfully belonging beside the thirteen that had won nationhood by the Revolution. Hitched tandem to "Free Trade and Sailors' Rights," the War

Hawks made a strong team with which to pull Mr. Madison's coach of state into an advantageous war. That the harness was too weak for such a rig was ignored by the majority of a Congress bent on fighting.

The New England Federalists, doing a fine trade with maritime Canada and the British army in Iberia, would have nothing to do with "Mr. Madison's War." The governors of the New England states even ignored the President's appeal of April 1812 to call out the militia. New England remained a set brake on the rear wheels of the nation and was dragged, squealing and protesting, through all the years of the war.

In an unsuccessful move to win New England, President Madison had appointed a New Hampshire man to lead the Army of the United States. During the Revolution, Major General Henry Dearborn had been a hero of such stature that he had assumed the proportions of a monument in the states east of the Hudson River. As a Jeffersonian Republican, Dearborn had died in all but affectionate memory of his great deeds. As Secretary of War during the administrations of President Jefferson, his work and influence had been minimal. The army was an insignificant thing, its budget an instrument of politics. Local governors supplied the labor to build strong coastal forts that an aggressor from the sea conceivably might attack. By 1812 there were some seventy-five stone forts or batteries mounting seven hundred and fifty guns, crouched, ready and waiting, on headlands, islands, and sand spits in most of the nation's ports. But in 1812 they were silent places, where the steps of caretakers echoed hollowly through the silent galleries and empty barracks. Occasionally militiamen in their gaudy uniforms came to exercise and strut in the forts if, as in New York City, the battery was convenient to the coffee house. Of the twelve thousand six hundred regulars who would be needed to man the system, less than half that number were available, and most of these were garrisoning the log stockades scattered through the west.

When Major General Dearborn eased his massive frame into his office chair, he had a fine array of regiments to parade across the flat top of his writing table. A frightened Congress had created additional regiments during the *Leopard* crisis of 1807, and it had neglected to rescind the enabling law when Jefferson shifted over to a war of embargo. The War Hawks who had favored Dearborn in January at the same time had bountifully authorized fourteen additional regiments. These regiments did not exist. Though amply provided for on paper, the sixty-one-year-old commander of the army had only some four thousand soldiers on the ground to begin the campaign that he had planned for the spring, if or when war was declared.

General Dearborn was virtually alone in his office. He had no staff of officers to translate the list of regiments on his desk into ranks of trained and equipped soldiers ready for battle. He had planned to liberate Canada by setting up an enveloping attack by armies from Detroit and Niagara to bite off western Canada and to draw the British troops away from the main American force that Dearborn himself would lead against Montreal from Lake Champlain. But he had no field commanders to carry out that plan. In his efforts the old general was aided by an enthusiastic Congress, a willing President, and a populace that everywhere, except in his native New England, cried for war. Even ex-President Jefferson predicted that

Canada would soon fall to American arms. No one noticed Mr. Madison's continued diplomatic pressure to get the British Orders in Council revoked and the French Decrees rescinded. That France had given in and that in London the Orders were canceled were facts that were ignored in the feverish excitement of a Congress set on war. "Free Trade and Sailors' Rights" was the cry as the ships sailed out and the armies marched to begin the conquest, the liberation, and the annexation of Canada.

XIII

The Frontiers of War

William Hull, governor of Michigan Territory, passed the winter of 1812 in Washington City. Even the new capital, damp, raw, half-built, and overcrowded, was preferable to Detroit, a drafty fort on a remote river and a mean town where French was the predominant tongue and the warehouses smelled of green pelts. At fifty-nine, Hull was in the comfortable years of life. In seven major battles of the Revolution, he had fought well as a regimental officer without distinguishing himself by any virtue other than competence. A postwar political career brought William Hull pedestrian success in his home state of Massachusetts. A place on an Indian Commission to Canada was an additional reward on a wider scale that, along with political loyalty, later qualified him for his appointment by Jefferson in 1805 to the governorship of the new territory of Michigan. Six years in the city of Detroit was a long stint for a gregarious man such as Hull.

For a man with friends, Washington City was a good place to be that exciting winter of 1812. On a fine day one could stand and watch the workmen raising the new halls of Congress, or one could listen as its members paved the way for the nation's steps to war. Dolly Madison was in the President's palace with her husband. The President's wife bore watching by the attentive and the wise. Henry Dearborn was appointed general, and the old veterans, in the taverns keeping out the chill, approved and hoped that their own appointment to brigades and departments and even regiments would now follow. William Hull had fought at Saratoga and Monmouth with General Dearborn, but he neither sought nor wanted military rank. Hull was content to leave the active command to younger men, men like his nephew Isaac, captain of the fine U.S. frigate *Constitution,* then in Chesapeake Bay. The governor of Michigan, however, had a place of importance in this society by the Potomac and frequently was called upon by the President for his opinion and advice.

In the square stone mansion then called the President's palace, William Hull talked to James Madison as one Jeffersonian Republican to another. The governor talked to the President about the defense of his territory, pointing out Michigan's vulnerability to British-inspired Indian attack from inland. From his chair facing President Madison, Governor Hull pointed out the dominance of Lake Erie by the British fleet and reiterated his plea for the American navy's presence there in strength. In his interview with the President, Governor Hull was most cautious about attempting to attack Canada from Michigan. Retaliation by Britain from the water and by the Indians from the forest would bring disaster to Detroit and to the scant thousand white American citizens there and on Mackinac Island. The President listened with a sympathetic ear, but all he heard and heeded was the cry of the War Hawks.

In March 1812 the elderly governor, who saw only failure in a second war with Britain, was offered a brigadier general's commission and the command of the army that was to invade Canada from Michigan. Hull demurred, but, on being pressed, he accepted the commission and the command. He did not spring to duty, as he had once charged so eagerly behind the compelling Wayne, up, over, and into the British fort at Stony Point. For six weeks Brigadier General William Hull tarried, while spring came to Washington City and while the army he was to command gathered and awaited his coming at the rendezvous in southern Ohio.

If Hull's reaction to his call to arms was dilatory and apathetic, that of Governor Return Jonathan Meigs of Ohio was not. The son and namesake of a father who had marched to Quebec with Arnold, Governor Meigs promptly executed his orders to supply an army for Hull. The Secretary of War had written him in March, asking that twelve hundred militiamen be assembled at Dayton to go with the governor of Michigan to Detroit. The militiamen, as eager as their governor to make war against Canada, turned out with enthusiasm. From a state muster of thirty thousand militiamen Meigs selected twelve hundred of the best, and they, the envied elite, formed themselves into three regiments and elected their colonels, and majors, and company officers, in the best tradition of free democratic Americans. Through most of May the Ohio militia waited in a high spirit of purpose that made light of their lack of creature comforts which, although expected, did not come. On his leisurely journey west General Hull organized his procurement and supply service. He arrived at Dayton on 25 May, thrice welcome: for himself, for the supplies he brought, and for the imminent departure his presence portended. The Ohio militiamen approved of the fine looking white-haired old gentleman who was their commander. When he spoke to them at the formal ceremony that gave them into his care the Ohio men were charmed. He spoke to them in the ringing oratory so dear to the hearts of western men. He spoke eloquently of Indian raids, and in fine phrases he excoriated England, the perfidious employer of savages against Christians. The men in the ranks nodded their agreement at each telling point in the general's peroration and cheered him loudly when, with becoming modesty, Hull indicated that his speech was over and action could begin. Behind the ranks upon ranks of soldiers, William Hull's daughter-in-law held up the children one by one, the better to see grandfather on his big horse.

On 1 June Governor Meigs bade farewell to Governor Hull and watched as the Ohioans marched up the road to Urbana. At that frontier post the one-hundred-and-seventy mile march through the wilderness to Detroit would begin in earnest. The governors had agreed that a trunk road must be built, both to bind the territory to the state, and to be used immediately in the present campaign. Although President Madison had responded to Hull's request by appointing a naval commissioner for Lake Erie, Commander Stewart, U.S.N., could not gain supremacy over the British fleet in time to aid the army that summer of 1812. So the town of Urbana would be the

starting point of the expedition, and on its dusty street General
Hull would meet the regiment of regular infantry that had
been allotted to his army.

From the forts along the Wabash the soldiers of the 4th
Regiment of Infantry gathered at Vincennes. The winter was
over, they were all together again, and the nation needed them
in far-off Michigan. They were ready to go. The citizens of
Indiana wished them Godspeed all down the river. Throughout northern Kentucky the people turned out to see and cheer
the veterans of Harrison's victory going by. The regiment
recrossed the Ohio River at Cincinnati, where they paraded
under an arch that proclaimed them "The Heroes of Tippecanoe." Beyond the city the regiment continued its route of
march until it neared Urbana. Outside of town it was met by
the three colonels of the Ohio militia, sent as an escort of honor
over the last mile. At the entrance to the main street the
soldiers could see another triumphal arch. This one was an
elaborate affair of intertwined evergreen boughs surmounted
by a rustic eagle. As they marched under the arch the soldiers
of the 4th saw the label, "Tippecanoe–Glory."

The pomp attending the arrival of the veterans was not lost
on the friendly Indians who had joined Hull's army for the
march north. As the way of the march to Detroit passed
through Indian land, the two governors had been most
punctilious in gaining permission for the march and for the
building of the road, and the Indians had been equally formal
in granting consent. Except for isolated raids and killings
further west, the Indians were quiet and neutral that spring.
The army marching north was expected to awe the red men

into continued peace and stop those isolated raids, which both sides ignored in their talks together.

Internal compromises, too, had to be arrived at before the expedition could set out as a united army on a common venture. The protocol of command had to be arranged with as much care and attention as the mess waiter gave to setting the general's table service. By the laws of the state of Ohio, the three colonels of militia carried their seniority in grade with them into federal service. Colonel James Miller, acting commander of the 4th, being but a lieutenant colonel, was therefore by Ohio law relegated to fourth in command after the general. Miller protested the downgrading of his federal commission, and he protested his competence as a trained and experienced professional soldier. General Hull, caught in a legal tangle for which he was unprepared, referred the whole affair back to Washington City for clarification. Miller accepted the compromise by delay, but the old difference between regulars and militia, inherited from colonial times, ruffled the smooth surface of amity at the senior table before the first meal was served.

There was trouble among the soldiers, too. A company of Ohio militiamen refused to march until they received certain pay to which they were entitled but which General Hull had no authority to grant. Colonel Miller, who, as a regular, recognized a mutiny at its first sneeze, marched in a company of the 4th and hauled out the three instigators. A court quickly condemned and sentenced the three to ignominy and discharge. General Hull, after due deliberation, exercised his prerogative to pardon with a magnanimity calculated to restore unity to the army. Work, hard work, building the long road north would further smooth over the discord that was apparent at the outset of the march.

Colonel Duncan McArthur with his 1st Ohio Regiment began the road. He was four days ahead of the last wagon in the train, which did not quit Urbana until the afternoon of 15 June. Colonel McArthur, who had been born in New York, followed only the blazes and the marks cut by the rangers, and the brisk old man of seventy who knew the best overland route to Detroit. It was the trail the old man followed when he drove his swine to the northern market. Forty miles up the new road, the 2nd Ohio, led by Colonel John Findlay, took over the brush hooks, the axes, the saws, and the labors of McArthur's men. Findlay's section of the road, through Wyandot country, crossed the low watershed that divided the Ohio River system from the basin of the Great Lakes. It was raining, and it rained for four days. In the moist heat of late June the mosquitoes swarmed, and the tiny black flies lived up to their name, "all jaws." At the head of the long column the insects plagued the road builders at their cutting and digging. At the rear of the column they pestered the flesh of the beeves being driven forward up the quagmire of the road. Following behind the main body of troops, three days behind the trail blazers, the wagon train was in trouble. Mud holes dragged at the wheels, axles broke, carts overturned, and the struggling horses and oxen gave out under the work of hauling. Laboriously, the carters and the baggage guard loaded the precious stores on the animals in packs and dragged and shoved and beat the failing beasts on up the road.

The sore-tried army came at last to Fort Findlay, built by

the 2nd Ohio on the forks of a river that ran into the Maumee. There, without rest, thirty-year-old Colonel Lewis Cass took over the road-building. His 3rd Ohioans' route ran across the Black Swamp, to the old abandoned British Fort Miami that Anthony Wayne's horsemen had taunted.

At Fort Findlay the army rested, while the pack animals grazed. On 26 June a courier from Washington City came posting up the road on a mud-spattered horse. He found General Hull in his tent by Sweetwater Creek and delivered the letter. Its message was short: General Hull was urged to hasten on to Detroit, where the army would wait for further orders. The paper that William Hull turned in his hand had been dated nine days before in Washington City on the morning of 18 June 1812. It said nothing more. The courier, last in a long line of messengers, had nothing to add, no news, no gossip. He had just taken the written message handed to him and had ridden on.

In quiet order, neither lax nor overly alert, the army moved on. The general was busy. From Fort Findlay much of the baggage could be moved by Indian canoe. He paid off many of the hired wagoners and hired friendly Indians. The roadmaking was easier with lighter traffic to bear. Cass's men built a blockhouse at the rapids of the Maumee which the army passed, after two days' marching through to Black Swamp. On 29 June the army made camp, across the Maumee from the battleground of Fallen Timbers. From the little settlement of American and French at the foot of the rapids, General Hull's niece and nephew turned out to welcome their uncle and cousins back to the territory of Michigan.

On 1 July while the Hull family and the army were still on

the Maumee, the privately owned schooner, *Cayauga,* out of Buffalo, sailed into the river. General Hull seized the opportunity she presented by chartering her for a trip to Detroit. The captain took $60 for the run. On the *Cayauga*'s deck, into her cabin, and into her hold went the heaviest baggage of the army, some of the sick, five army wives, two boys, and, last, the bandsmen with their instruments. General Hull sent along his personal baggage, including his brassbound field desk, its pigeon holes neatly stuffed with private papers, parade states, sick reports, inventories of stores, and the private and confidential orders from the capital in Washington. The *Cayauga* sailed on the same day in company with a small open boat that had also been engaged for the trip past the British forts to Detroit.

Unencumbered now, the army moved out on the last leg of its journey. There were roads already built linking the Maumee settlements to that at the River Raisin, Brownstown beyond, and along the west bank of the Detroit River to Detroit. It was the 4th Regiment's turn to lead, and this they did in tactical order. Hull had received reports that the Wyandot were defiant and that Tecumseh was out with fifteen hundred warriors behind him. Hull expected their attack near Brownstown, where two hundred Sioux had been seen.

The army was away from the Maumee on the evening of 1 July when Hull ordered his tent to be pitched for the night. The elderly general was roused from his cot shortly after midnight. A letter had just come in from Cleveland, on Lake Erie. The letter, in an official packet from Washington City, addressed to General Hull at Detroit, had arrived at Cleveland by ordinary post. Though the face of the letter bore no instructions indicating urgency, the Cleveland postmaster was reluctant to toss such an important-looking letter onto the pile waiting for the next boat to Detroit. On his own initiative, the postmaster hired a young local man to ride special post to the army, which was believed to be at or approaching the west end of Lake Erie. So at last, after much handling and delay, the letter was delivered to Hull. By the light of a watch lantern hung on the tent post, the general read the short message. "War is declared against Great Britain." There followed a few terse instructions: Hurry to Detroit, make ready, be on guard, use your own judgment, and wait for further orders.

The letter that General Hull received in the early hours of 2 July, and the message he received by special courier a week before, were both dated from Washington City on 18 June. That was the day on which, after two weeks of hard politicking by the War Hawks, the President had made his declaration of war. If the government had been dilatory about getting the news to an army commander approaching danger in ignorance, General Hull was equally casual about spreading the word. Hull did not alert either Fort Wayne or Fort Dearborn to the west or even Detroit and Mackinac to the north. He did try with frantic haste to stop the *Cayauga* before she cleared the mouth of the Maumee. The horseman was too late; the schooner and her consort were in the big lake.

On the morning of 2 July the *Cayauga*, her captain, and all on board learned that they were at war with Canada. About to pass Fort Amherst, and the brig *General Hunter* with her guns run out, the *Cayauga* was stopped by a longboat, and Lieutenant Charles Rolette of the Provincial Marines came over the side. With a gesture toward the cannon, he informed all on board that they were prisoners of war and that the ship and stores were, of course, forfeit to the Crown. Standing on the quarterdeck of his prize, Lieutenant Rolette ordered her in shore to an anchorage and commanded the startled bandsmen to break out their instruments to play the vessel in. The tune he chose was "God Save the King." The little open boat, which had fallen behind the *Cayauga* during the night, took the east channel for an uneventful passage up to Detroit, where a state of peace in ignorance still existed.

Although no official word had come from London to Canada, Governor General Sir George Prevost was well informed of the fever for war building up below his southern border. The British ambassador to the United States had informed him that the House of Representatives had voted for war on 4 June and that the Senate was sure to add the necessary approval. On this advice Prevost began to prepare for the defense of Montreal and ordered Isaac Brock to do the same in Upper Canada. Prevost did not need the proof of a battle-damaged frigate limping into Halifax with her dead and wounded to know that war had begun. The New York agent of the Northwest Fur Company had been sent to Quebec expressly to alert the company in Canada that war had been declared, and to discuss its commercial implications. The Northwest's man in Quebec immediately passed on the news to Governor General Prevost. Brock, too, had his contacts with the business world. John Jacob Astor, the American, whose fur interests reached far into Canada, had sent the news west from Albany, so General Brock had heard of the war on 24 June. Lieutenant Colonel Thomas St. George, commanding at Fort Amherst, was alerted on 28 June and reacted promptly. He sent a detachment of troops to Sandwich, opposite Detroit, to close down the ferry and to watch the Yankees. Colonel St. George, with the help of the Provincial Marine, seized all the American shipping he could lay hold of in the Detroit River. Two of the boats he took were carrying food to the American army, whose approach the colonel was watching. The British commander on the Detroit River was careful in his confiscation. Without specific orders he dared not board, search, and confiscate any U.S. government vessel. So he let a revenue cutter with the strangely striped flag of its service glide peacefully under the guns of Fort Amherst and the brig. But the merchantman *Cayauga,* coming upstream an hour after the cutter passed, was fair game, and General William Hull's desk, full of his most confidential papers, made any risk of an overt, hostile act worthwhile for the colonel.

To the elderly governor of Michigan, suddenly a general at war, haste spelled caution. There was a bridge to be built. Care must be taken lest the Wyandot Indians or the dread Tecumseh lay in ambush. The English might attack the army strung out in line of march. Finally, when Detroit was just ahead, General Hull stopped his army to permit his troops to wash out their clothing, filthy from the march. The general's dragging steps generated the friction of discontent among the eager militiamen from Ohio. The officers and men remembered Hull's fiery oratory at Dayton, where they had mustered under the banner of their general's silver hair and thrilled to the golden promise of victory over the Canadians. Hull's fine words, which had been a squealing fife tune to action, were now but the thumping drumbeat of a white-haired old man repeating the orders he himself had received, "Wait for further orders." The regular soldiers of the 4th Regiment of Infantry kept themselves aloof. They sought out the ninety soldiers of another regiment to cement a professional bond and to learn the ways and byways of this new town. The men of the 4th made their appraisal of Detroit. They looked across the river to the foreign shore to which, soon enough, they would be sent to do the familiar work for which they had come over such a long road.

XIV

The Invaluable Blessing of Liberation

The invasion of Canada began on 12 July 1812 with a boat ride and a salvo of bombast. In the morning all of the troops crossed over the Detroit River. They stepped gingerly onto the strange foreign land that neither felt nor looked in any way different from the Detroit shore from which they had come. Deploying quickly, the regulars, followed by the Ohioans, secured and passed through the Canadian town of Sandwich. Some of the hurrying soldiers noticed the shattered boards of the Huron church, damaged in the exchange of cannon shots that a week before had announced the beginning of hostilities. By noon General Hull was ensconced in his headquarters in a fine brick house at the edge of the town. So far the invasion had been quiet, no shots fired, and only two British officers seen and they had galloped off at the approach of the boats. In the anteroom at headquarters, Hull's aides were busy ripping open the bundles of printed proclamations, scatter-shot aimed at the gentle hearts of the loyal Canadian people.

Colonel Cass had written the document in fine prose, soft as rolling smoke yet hard as a cast cannon ball. The invading Americans came not to conquer, but to liberate. In promising prosperity, he guaranteed the "invaluable blessing of civil, political, and religious liberty." The warnings of retribution that followed the phrases offering freedom were hard and telling. "An indiscriminate scene of desolation" would follow any rising of the Indians, and "instant destruction" would be meted out to any Canadian found fighting with the savages. Almost blandly, the proclamation mentioned that the Americans had the force to "look down all opposition" to the liberation of the Canadians.

The fine effect of Cass's bombast was immediately apparent in Sandwich. The French turned out with smiles on their faces and their children ran after the soldiers marching past the damaged church. Hull could expect an even better response, and some volunteers, from the countryside around Lake St. Clair and up the fair valley of the Thames. Many Americans had settled in farms and communities there; among them was Hull's younger brother, Isaac. Meanwhile the troops were marching toward Fort Malden and Amherstburg, the seat of Britain's power. Once the fort and town were reduced by Hull's cannon, the Indians would be malleable, the threat to Detroit removed, half of Upper Canada liberated, and Hull's orders from Washington City successfully executed. On the first day of the invasion General Hull's new orders, although peremptory and unequivocable: "Commence operations immediately," seemed easy to execute.

On the second day the dread savages were reported everywhere. A captain of Findlay's regiment, scouting and distributing proclamations nine miles toward Amherstburg, almost encountered Tecumseh himself in woods that he reported were full of prowling Indians. A mounted patrol sent along to the south shore of Lake St. Clair heard that a war party of one hundred Indians was skulking in the neighborhood. Besieged now, and beset with caution, General Hull reacted with conservatism. He called the army back to fortify the camp at Sandwich, to protect the short line of retreat back to Detroit, and to wait on the making of traveling carriages for the siege guns that he would need to "possess" Fort Malden, in accordance with his orders. Consistent with those orders, General Hull must also keep ever in mind the "safety of the American posts"—meaning Detroit.

The eager offensive spirit of the Ohio colonels was difficult for the old general to quench. Colonel McArthur won permission to take a force of one hundred men and cavalry to drive the band of Indians away from Lake St. Clair. The war party was quickly dispersed, and McArthur, with a bundle of proclamations in his aide's saddle bag, continued up the valley of the Thames. He did not return to Sandwich until 17 July, when he brought in commandeered boats, flour, blankets, whisky, and some few military stores, and a very few volunteers. Behind him McArthur left a poor plundered people who for a brief moment had believed Hull's proclamation of their liberty.

In the opposite direction from the fortified camp at Sandwich Colonel Cass was winning the title of "Hero of Tarontée" by disobeying Hull's orders. Sent to view the bridge over the Aux Canards or Tarontée River, but not to cross over, Cass saw that it was held by a small detachment of British soldiers. Though ordered not to cross the marsh and stream, young Cass was off and running wide like a bird dog

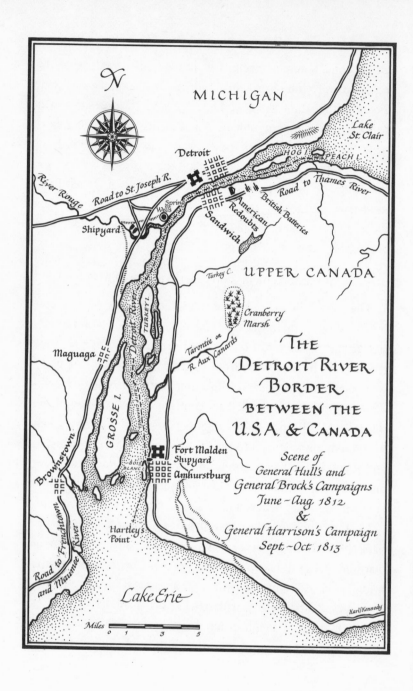

THE
DETROIT RIVER
BORDER
BETWEEN THE
U.S.A. & CANADA

Scene of
General Hull's and
General Brock's Campaigns
June – Aug. 1812
&
General Harrison's Campaign
Sept. – Oct. 1813

Karl Kennedy

MICHIGAN

Lake St. Clair

Detroit

HOG I. PEACH I.

River Rouge

Road to St. Joseph R.

Road to Thames River

Spring Wells

American Redoubts

British Batteries

Shipyard

Sandwich

Turkey C.

UPPER CANADA

Cranberry Marsh

Detroit River

Tarontee or R. Aux Canards

TURKEY I.

Maguaga

GROSSE I.

N.W. CHANNEL

Brownstown

BOIS BLANC I.

Fort Malden
Shipyard
Amhurstburg

Hartley's Point

Road to Frenchtown and Maumee River

Lake Erie

Miles
0 1   3   5

circling down wind. While riflemen fixed the enemy at the
bridge Cass crossed well up the Tarontée and came back down
on the British side. When he got to the bridge he found that
the riflemen had driven off the enemy. Cass pursued for a mile
down the road, but realizing that he was only three miles from
an alerted Fort Malden, he stopped abruptly and ordered a return to the bridge. There he found his riflemen tending two
wounded prisoners, one of whom, identified by his mate as Private Hancock of the 41st, was dying.

With a vital bridge and causeway in his hands, Cass called
on Hull for reinforcements and eagerly prepared to defend and
hold the prize that he had won. The 4th Regiment came up to
the bridge with a field piece on 17 July, with orders from Hull
to confer with Lieutenant Colonel Miller of the regulars as to
the wisdom of holding a bridge in such an advanced position
with a vulnerable water flank. To avoid conferring with an
officer junior to himself, Colonel Cass took a vote among all
the officers. The consensus, by the democratic process, was
overwhelmingly to return to Sandwich. Colonel Cass reluctantly returned to camp to pout over the injustice done him
and the victory snatched away. It was the press who much
later inflated the action into a battle and the principal actor into
"The Hero of Tarontée."

Both of the other Ohio colonels had orders to have a look at
Cass's bridge. Findlay found it torn up and the 18-gun *Queen
Charlotte* anchored bow and stern to give covering fire.
McArthur, too, found the British in strength at the bridge and
Indians patrolling the woods. Cass joined McArthur, and
together they made a display which satisfied the Ohioans' pride

and flaunted their general's orders not to tempt an engagement.

Two of Hull's colonels had now been insubordinate and the third stood with his comrades. All three were for the quick thrust through to Fort Malden, and each passing day of indecision seemed to them an opportunity lost. Frustration nurtured discouragement, and idleness turned gossip into slander. Ohioans set William Hull down as a coward, and some from behind their hand suspected that their general planned treachery. Had not his own brother been a Canadian since 1804? The best they could say, when General Hull went over to Detroit taking the outranked Miller with him, was that the two had gone on frivolous business.

In point of fact, General Hull had gone back to Detroit to hurry the making of the cannon carriages, which would not be ready for another two weeks. Hull was anxious, too, about his overland supply route, which from the Maumee to Detroit passed close to Fort Malden and across which lay the Wyandot town of Brownstown. For four days General Hull remained in his house in Detroit. At Sandwich, Colonel McArthur, left in command, suffered the first Americans killed in action. In a routine patrol toward the tempting Tarontée bridge, one hundred-odd Ohioans bumped into a party of Indians in a wood near Turkey Creek. Surprised and disorganized, the militiamen milled about in confusion, crying alarm. When the Indians withdrew in order they left one of their own dead, for the three Americans sprawled lifeless on the ground. On their sad walk back to Sandwich carrying their dead, the Americans came upon the body of Rifleman Avery Powers. Him, too, they bore along to the fortified bridgehead to await the return of the general and, perhaps, a revitalization of the dragging campaign.

The action near Turkey Creek brought special praise from General Brock for the Indians engaged. The lieutenant governor of Upper Canada, however, was unable to go himself to threatened Amherstburg until 13 August. As president and administrator, Isaac Brock had to be at his capital at York, prepared and ready to open the provincial legislature. He had anticipated a difficult session. The opposition was plainly sympathetic to the American cause, while the neutrals and those apathetic to the war had been impressed or overawed by General Hull's proclamation. Governor Brock's own counter-proclamation won support from the people, and with this and his own force of personality, he won a War Supplies Bill from his legislature. He then prorogued the parliament and turned promptly from politics to the less bitter acts of open warfare conceived for the defense of the province. Brock's tactical plan was to strike quickly, to capture Fort Niagara before the Americans could build up an army there and on the river border. His strategic intent was to throw the Yankees' offensive plan off balance along Upper Canada's most vulnerable frontier. But a higher authority, with lofty political motives, forestalled General Brock's plan, which in the first two months of war gave every indication of success. Sir George Prevost, the governor general of both Canadas and of the Maritime Provinces, though a general, was a political man. As such he saw in the anti-war feeling of the New England Federalists a hope that a divided United States would defeat itself before it could attack a militarily weak Canada. A Canadian invasion such as Brock planned would only solidify the war spirit of the Americans and turn the declared war into a crusade. Then too, there was a possibility, realized even then, but still not known in Quebec, that the Orders in Council might be revoked. With that cause for war removed, peace might be a reality before the real battle for North America was even joined. Prevost ordered Brock to remain on Canadian soil at Niagara in a purely passive defense. With this command in effect, General Brock could give his attention and his presence to the Detroit frontier, where the enemy stood defiant on Canadian soil. He had already done what he could to support his threatened commander at Fort Malden.

Lieutenant Colonel Thomas St. George, detached from the 63rd Foot, had sat his horse watching as the American invasion fleet drew nearer and nearer to the Canadian shore on the morning of 12 July. When the boats drew close he wheeled and, with his aide cantering behind him, rode away, abandoning but not surrendering that part of Upper Canada. Colonel St. George was over-all commander of western Upper Canada, and his work that morning had just begun. Sandwich and the country around had been shucked bare of provender and the last loaded wagons and straggling flocks and herds were moving slowly on the road to amherstburg. St. George chivvied them on their way with the last of the militiamen who had answered the lieutenant governor's call to arms. At Amherstburg about three hundred militiamen had already gathered to train and prepare to fend off an American attack. Fort Malden, a well-sited modern fort, was the depot of the 41st Foot and the garrison gunners of the Royal Artillery. When the war began Captain Adam Muir and his one hundred and fifty man company of regulars were, with the gunners, the only occupants of the fort. Colonel Henry Procter soon would be coming with another one hundred and fifty men of the regiment, but when Colonel St. George rode back into his strong point at the end of invasion day, he had but four hundred and fifty men under arms.

These few did not, however, reflect the strength given the defenders by the navy. The Provincial Marines' dockyard at Amherstburg was home port for the vessels of war *Queen Charlotte, General Hunter,* and *Lady Prevost,* all formidable rulers of the inland seas, and monarchs of the routes of supply and movement over the lakes' surface. In addition to these warships, which the Americans could match only by *Adams,* then in dry dock below Detroit, four Northwest Company vessels of fifty tons or more were available for service to the Crown.

The act of submission of Tecumseh to the Crown, in the days of anxious rumor before the declaration of war, was a potential of defense that was soon to prove its worth to the commander of Malden and Amherstburg, faced with the fact of invasion and the imminent possibility of attack and siege. A hundred and fifty warriors and their families had followed Tecumseh into exile. Neither they nor their leader had come to the British for sanctuary. To Britain they had submitted as co-belligerents, temporarily beaten allies wanting a chance to draw breath and then strike again. In Fort Malden Britain provided a sanctuary for them, and Matthew Elliott, now Deputy Superintendent of Indian Affairs, provided them the means to retaliate. But Tecumseh accepted Britain's aid as his due. He was aloof, arrogant, sure among the lesser men, St. George, Muir, Procter, and Elliott, whom he had come to help. From the Indian camp on Bois Blanc Island, across the main channel from Amherstburg, Tecumseh led his band out along the land flank of the river road to Sandwich. His Indians crossed single file on the bare timbers of Tarontée bridge to harass and annoy the Yankee flank and pester the great camp opposite Detroit. More Indians came from many nations, and Tecumseh, a natural leader, took them under his direction.

As the momentum of Hull's invasion bogged down on the Canadian side of the river, Tecumseh struck on the American shore. The main road from the Maumee to Detroit ran on the west shore of the Niagara River. Opposite Fort Malden, behind the southern point of Grosse Isle, was the village of Brownstown. Tecumseh himself was there on the morning of 5 August with twenty-four warriors and Matthew Elliott's son in Indian dress. The Shawnee chief had another band watching the road to the south.

Tecumseh drew first blood. A mail convoy for Ohio with an escort of two hundred of Findlay's regiment under command of a major were on the road that morning. Tecumseh's scouts saw the Americans well north of Brownstown, and they did not resist the temptation to kill two, an Ohio captain and a Negro soldier, riding point through a cornfield. Though warned, the American major blundered on into Tecumseh's ambush. In the short sharp fire fight and the controlled pursuit of the fleeing American force, Tecumseh's Indians shot with deliberate discrimination. They killed six officers and ten privates that day. They took the wagon with the letters for home, and two prisoners, but, before Tecumseh could stop them, the Indians killed the Americans, in revenge for their Chief Logan, the only Indian who died that day.

The war party watching the road south of Brownstown also

captured mail. They ambushed a small mounted patrol carrying letters from Ohio, in advance of a big supply column waiting at the Maumee Rapids for the escort that Tecumseh had turned back.

The Indians, by interposing themselves between General Hull and his much needed supplies, had tactically isolated the American army, but, even more, the information that the British gleaned from the captured mail gave them a strategic superiority by which they could go over to the offensive. Letter after letter, as they were opened and read in the orderly room at Fort Malden, told of the dissatisfaction and distrust felt by the Ohio militia for their general. Man after man expressed disenchantment and anger at William Hull's inaction. Mutiny was nearer with each reported instance of Hull's refusal to listen to his colonels. Discouragement was written in the crabbed hand of privates and in the eloquent phrases of officers, telling the people at home of the needless loss of the American fort at Mackinac, lost only because General Hull had neglected to send word that war had been declared.

XV

General Hull's Michigan

Captain Charles Roberts of the British army considered it his duty to tell Lieutenant Porter Hanks of the American army that they were enemies. The two officers were neighbors, separated by fifty miles of often rough water at the upper end of Lake Huron. The Englishman commanded at the new British fort on St. Joseph Island, guarding the portage to Lake Superior, the valuable locks and canal, and the warehouses of the Northwest Fur Company. From his fort on Mackinac Island the American officer commanded the Straits of Mackinac to Lake Michigan and the warehouses of the Northeast Fur Company, which was the American-owned subsidiary of the "Nor'westers." Captain Roberts did not know whether his Yankee neighbor had heard the news. On 16 July he set out across the water with an army at his back to tell Lieutenant Hanks in positive terms that they were at war. A Northeast Company man on his way to the spring fur rendezvous at Fort William at the lower end of Lake Superior had informed Captain Roberts of this fact on 8 July. Two days later General

Brock's messenger had officially verified the news of war. Two follow-up messengers had clarified the lieutenant governor's intent and the captain's orders, to take Mackinac from Lieutenant Hanks.

Roberts had begun his preparations for an amphibious attack on 8 July. To carry out Brock's anticipated order, the British captain had forty-five slightly sober soldiers of the 10th Royal Veteran Battalion. In eight days he had raised and launched his expedition of six hundred and twenty-five men. Driving their big canoes forward to the accompaniment of a crackling volubility of song and banter, were one hundred and eighty bandy-legged *voyageurs* of the Northwest Company, armed and organized. They were McGillivray's men, as were the four hundred painted Indians pulling their light canoes swiftly across the roiled water. William McGillivray, "Lord of the Northwest," had prepared the Indians for war, and they followed his bidding, Sioux, Ojibway, Menomee, Winnebago, and Ottawa. On board the company brig *Caledonia,* sailing with a bone in her teeth, Captain Roberts cajoled his besotted Redcoats for the landing next morning. A 6-pound cannon, dismantled and trussed ready to go ashore, lay dumb on the brig's deck.

At three o'clock on the morning of 17 July, the British expeditionary force touched down on Mackinac Island at a place considerably distant from Lieutenant Hanks's well-gunned fort on a high bluff. By first light the 6-pounder was assembled, charged and emplaced on a hill. Over its gleaming barrel the gun captain had a fair sight into the American fort. He could see the bluecoated soldiers hurrying to assembly and all the fort's cannon mounted to bear on the lake beyond.

From every loophole through which Lieutenant Hanks peered the view was the same. On every side painted savages and wild *voyageurs* waited in little groups for the fiery wink of the cannon's eye to begin their attack. The civilians in the harborside village were cut off from view by a dip in the land. All seemed quiet in that direction, but the threat of massacre lay in the glint of the rising sun on the blades of bayonets, tomahawks, and spearpoints. In all that ominous mob only the orderly block of redcoated soldiers, the gunners ranged around their piece, and the little staff group around Captain Roberts looked friendly to the surrounded lieutenant of U.S. artillery. With a drum tapping slowly and a white flag limp on an upheld stick the British staff party marched down the hill to seek a parley. Lieutenant Porter Hanks welcomed the party at the half-opened gate and there learned that for a month his country and Britain had been at war. Helpless in his ignorance, Hanks surrendered his fort, his troops, his government stores, and his island. Captain Roberts kept his wild band in order. There was no pillaging, looting, scalping to mar the transfer of Mackinac Island to British sovereignty.

In quiet order, the Indians of Roberts's command left him. They crossed over to the Michigan shore, turned south to follow the line of beaches and forested shore to the place where Tecumseh awaited their coming. In noise and confusion the Nor'westers returned to the fur routes to serve the pleasure, the profit, and the patriotism of the McGillivray. Down at the harbor, the sixty men of 1st U.S. artillery, transformed by defeat from soldiers to a huddled mob, waited on the deck of the vessel that would take them under cartel to Detroit.

As General Hull listened to the paroled Lieutenant Hanks

tick off on his fingers the names of the Indian nations that were
with the British at Mackinac Island, the territory which the old
governor administered shrank. Finally, when the young officer
was done, there was nothing left to the Territory of Michigan
that the guns of Fort Detroit could not cover with their fire.
Hull's daughter and the children in Government House would
be able to hear quite plainly in the still dawn the war cry of
Indians from the edge of the forest. By then the children
would be hungry, for the road to Ohio was cut and the supply
train waited an escort.

Beleaguered by Indians and the British from without,
General Hull was besieged by the Ohio colonels from within.
They demanded action. They had to have the supplies waiting
on the Maumee. Summoning all his awesome dignity, General
Hull refused to send the escort that would weaken the defenses
of the last pitiful bit of Michigan that was left him to govern.
Then, with the benevolence that marks a truly indecisive man,
Hull consented to send two hundred men to the Maumee with
the home mail, to return as escort with the supplies. It was this
party, under Major Thomas Van Horne, that fell into
Tecumseh's ambush near Brownstown.

The haggling between the colonels and the general continued. Once more General Hull was forced to compromise in
favor of the colonels; he agreed to launch at once the
long-delayed attack on Fort Malden. Thirty years before,
Hull, as a Major of Continentals, had made the bayonet attack
which carried Stony Point for "Mad Anthony Wayne." For
Fort Malden, Lieutenant Colonel Miller's 4th and the Detroit
detachment from the 1st Infantry were up to the control and
discipline of an assault with the bayonet. The Ohio militia,

untrained, individualistic, questioning, were not the tried Continentals of '79, but they were enthusiastic. Jubilantly, the officers and men in the beachhead made ready for the march down the Canadian shore. Before they could move General Hull changed his mind. A spy told him that General Brock himself was coming to Fort Malden with regulars, militia, and more Indians to attack Detroit from the land side. In the face of the new danger, Hull called off the attack and ordered the army back from across the Detroit River. They came in their boats, mumbling and grumbling through the long night of 7 August and into the following morning. By noon of 8 August only a token force of invalids and a few artillerymen remained in Canada, keeping a stone house that they called a fort but which was a tombstone of hope and a mark of shame.

Saved from a foolhardy attack and expecting a long siege, General Hull reconsidered a former firm decision. He had to send the strong escort to bring up the supply train still waiting at the Maumee Rapids. Hull gave the command of the six-hundred-man force to Lieutenant Colonel Miller, who was still submerged below the tossing waves made by three Ohio colonels.

The next day, 9 August, was sunny. Miller, who had left the fort at Detroit the afternoon before, was marching slowly to keep pace with the two cannon that he had taken with him. In mid-afternoon the advance guard came upon the body of one of the volunteer scouts. He was a man named White. He now lay scalped, stripped, and raw beside the empty cabin of the Wyandot chief Walk-In-The-Water. The advance guard were still gawking at the body as the cavalry, riding at a walk, came down the road. The infantry, in two columns, were marching through the open fields to the right and to the left. They marched alert to danger in the oak woods beyond their land flank. Leaving White's body, the advance guard hurried on toward the Wyandot village of Maguaga, deserted now that Walk-In-The-Water had taken his people over to Tecumseh on the British side.

The advance party, under Captain Josiah Snelling of the 4th, took the first sharp fusillade of the British and Indians, hidden in the oak woods. Miller soon came up to find the redheaded Snelling, hatless, supervising the deliberate return fire of veterans of Tippecanoe. The cannon were unlimbering the cannon as the infantry jogged up, their accouterments flapping. Without giving them pause, Colonel Miller turned columns into line with an order and charged the woods. The advance guard went with them. In the scrub growth between the big trees, the American line pushed on, neighbor calling to neighbor lest the line break. Of the enemy all they saw was the glimpse of a running redcoat or the painted back of a departing Indian. There was some unidentified musketfire from the riverbank, and from the road the men in the woods heard the reassuring thump of the American cannon. The charge slowed to a walk as Miller's soldiers cleared the woods of the enemy. For a brief interval the advance was held up by a pocket of Indians—Tecumseh's men. Of the British regulars and Canadian militia nothing was seen again.

On returning to the start line, Captain Snelling found Colonel Miller lying on the ground, all but senseless with shock and pain from a bad fall from his horse. Regulars and militiamen were bringing in the American wounded to the abandoned Indian huts of Maguaga. There were over sixty wounded, and, lying still on the trampled grass, eighteen dead, all in a line. Of the British and Indian dead and wounded no count could be taken. There were only vague reports of individuals who saw a body here or there in the woods. None of the American officers cared to count the scalps taken by their own men, though later a civilian in Detroit counted forty of these gory trophies.

But it was growing late in the day as the victorious army gathered and regrouped at Maguaga. The British had gone back across the river and the Indians had retreated deeper into their woods. Colonel Miller, sick, hurt, and scarcely rational, ordered his force to bivouac the night. The ever-eager Snelling was sent back to Detroit for aid for the wounded, supplies, and reinforcements. For thirty-six hours the injured Miller lay with his force at the battle site. Colonel McArthur came boldly up and took away the wounded. Colonel Cass mustered his regiment and sought permission from Hull to relieve the stricken regulars and continue the march to the Maumee. However, on 12 August General Hull ordered the whole force back to the safety of Detroit. The vital supplies could remain back at the Maumee Rapids. So tight was the Indian hoop around Hull's army that neither the general nor Colonel Miller knew that the supplies were only a day's march away from Maguaga, and that after the battle the road between was clear. Captain Henry Brush, tired of waiting, had moved his supply train to the River Raisin. There, with his own ranger cavalry and the militiamen of Frenchtown, he sat down to wait again the coming of the escort.

XVI

Two Days in August

Close on to midnight on 13 August 1812, *Queen Charlotte* dropped anchor in the roads off Fort Malden and Amherstburg. General Isaac Brock stood on the quarterdeck, ready to go ashore, while the sailors secured the vessel and brought the boat around to the gangway. Lights were coming up all over the town and a drum beat an assembly in the fort. Over on Bois Blanc Island a red flame leaped up where an Indian threw a bundle of twigs onto a dying fire. In the dark around the brig the other boats of the convoy were preparing to land the soldiers who had come with Brock to the threatened west. Three hundred of them were good men of the flank companies; the other forty were additional regulars of the 41st and the Royal Newfoundland Fencibles, come to join those sent on before with Procter.

General Brock waited for no dockside reception. He strode on to the fort at once, picking up the awakened senior officers as he went. He sent an aide to Tecumseh, requesting the Indian to join him at headquarters. In keeping with British policy, Brock had avoided the hiring of Indians, but Tecumseh could represent a government in exile and share with Britain the usurpation of its land by a common enemy. Brock wished to meet the Indian leader in the interest of the common defense and the future interest of both nations, faced with a common menace.

In the lamp-lit room Isaac Brock heard the reports and questioned his officers. Excerpts were read from the letters captured with the Detroit mail and now sorted and stacked on a side table. Brock then knew the condition and low morale of the American army against him, and he was learning the temper of his own officers grouped around him in the close room. Brock was forming his own plans and charting the course of his own leadership when the door opened and Tecumseh stepped into the light.

The Indian was dressed in fine buckskin from ankle to neck. A large silver medallion hung around his neck and three small crown-like ornaments dangled from the cartilage of his nose. He wore moccasins intricately worked with quills in design. His bearing was proud and his presence filled the crowded room. He remained apart from the others while he measured the stature of Isaac Brock. Tecumseh had already observed and judged St. George and Proctor and the grey-haired Muir, whose soldiers had not impressed the chief during the encounter at Walk-In-The-Water's town. Through the early hours of 14 August Tecumseh stood in the presence of Brock. At four in the morning, having heard all the valid reasons why he should not attack, General Brock announced his decision to attack Detroit at once. In the quiet that followed, all in that little room heard Tecumseh say: "This is a man." General Brock continued with his detailed orders.

On the day following a night of little rest, Brock addressed the brigade of Indians. He stood before the painted men, with Tecumseh their chief and their brigadier. While Brock spoke the British and Canadian troops, organized now into three brigades, were preparing to march toward Sandwich. The siege and field trains of guns, with all their attending wagons, were ready to roll by afternoon. Engineers had gone ahead to repair and reinforce the bridge over the Tarontée. In the river three vessels of the Provincial Marine were topping off ships' stores of food and ordnance materiel and taking on supplies that the army would need in the camp upriver.

By early afternoon of the following day, 15 August 1812, General Brock was ready to make the first of the planned offensive steps in his attack on the American army in Detroit. The troops were arriving in camp south of Sandwich. The fleet was discharging stores preparatory to assuming a gun role against the town. A five-gun siege battery was in place and were digging in on the shore opposite Detroit.

The first step in a siege is the formal request, in the name of humanity, to surrender. General Brock was a master at incorporating into his request all the power of shock and propaganda which is the true purpose of the formal exchange between enemies. He had already countered Hull's Proclamation of Canadian Liberation by his own appeal, which had restored most of the dissident Canadians to their true loyalty. The letter he sent across the Detroit River was simple but telling on a Yankee general and governor whom Brock knew to be indecisive, beset by enemies within, and rightfully apprehensive of an Indian massacre in Detroit. General Brock pointed out to General Hull that the British would lose control over Tecumseh's Indians if the Americans resisted and gave the red men cause for revenge. General Hull replied to General Brock with the expected punctilious refusal to surrender. An hour later, at four o'clock in the afternoon the British shore battery and the guns of *Queen Charlotte* and *General Hunter* opened fire on Detroit.

General William Hull heard the British guns, and he heard the American shore battery open up in reply. Even nearer, two 24-pounders, hastily emplaced in Judge August B. Woodward's garden, came noisily into action. The guns of the fort, unable to carry to the far shore or to the British vessels, remained silent, waiting their chance. Though Hull listened, and others on the walls of the fort and at the loopholes of the town stockade listened, there was no whooping or firing of muskets on the landward side. Tecumseh's Indians had not yet come for Detroit.

General Hull had abandoned even the pretense of the offensive on 11 August when he had brought back from the Canadian shore the last detachment of American soldiers. He was committed to defend Detroit and to wait for reinforcements. Hull had cried out for more troops. Secretary of War Eustis had replied that Governor Meigs would take responsibility for the security of the supply roads through Ohio, and that Brigadier General James Winchester was coming to Detroit with fifteen hundred Kentucky volunteers. Without the necessity to make decisions, it would be easy and comfortable to await the coming of the Kentuckians. But

Battle of the Thames:
Colonel Johnson's charge and death of Tecumseh

The confrontation of Governor Harrison and Tecumseh at Vincennes

Indian attack: Mrs. Heald at evacuation of Fort Dearborn

Fort Harrison on the Wabash River

Oliver Hazard Perry,
U. S. Navy

Colonel Richard M. Johnson,
Member of Congress

Brigadier General William Hull,
Governor of Michigan Territory

Major General William Henry
Harrison, Governor of Indiana
Territory, Hero of Tippecanoe

Tenskwatawa, "The Prophet"   Tecumseh

British Regulars storming Fort Stephenson

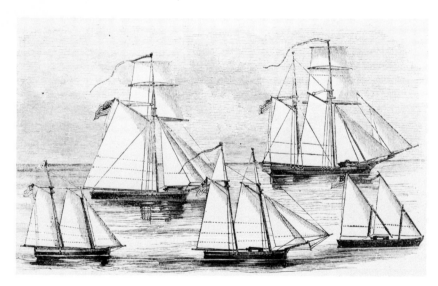

Gunboats

Indian ambush of General St. Clair

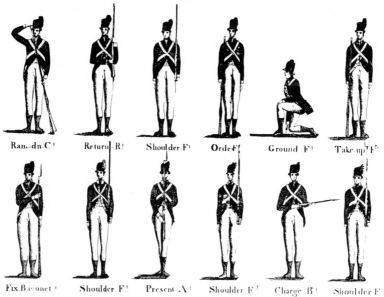

Ram-dn-C! Return-R! Shoulder-F! Orde-F! Ground F! Take-up F!

Fix Bayonet! Shoulder-F! Present A! Shoulder F! Charge B! Shoulder F!

U. S. Infantryman prior to 1801

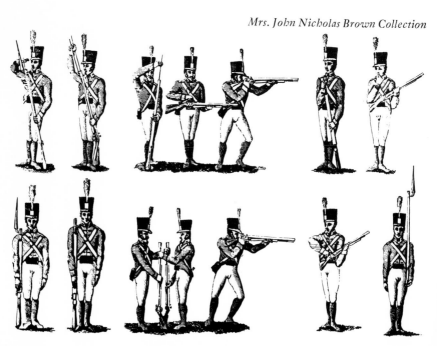

U. S. Infantryman 1813

though his perimeters were drawn and his troops assigned their defensive posts the Ohio colonels would give the old general no rest. Colonel Cass was in covert revolt. He was circulating a petition to arrest Hull and put the willing Colonel McArthur in supreme command. Every move the general made was suspect. They saw that he drank and was sleeping drunk. When the general had his marque raised south of the fort, its odd coloring, red and blue stripes, caused comment. Robert Lewis, a scout and Ohioan attached to McArthur, suspected that the tent was a signal displayed for the British. There were many who listened to Lewis's rumor and who spread their own stories.

Colonels McArthur and Cass were not at Detroit when the crescendo of crisis roared into the rumble of an artillery duel over the river. On 14 August Hull had sent the two malcontent conspirators on another attempt to bring up the stores from the River Raisin. For the next two days, the two colonels and four hundred of their most faithful militiamen were wandering in the woods out of contact with Fort Detroit, and unable to find the supply train which was supposedly making its way toward them. On Sunday, 16 August, McArthur's and Cass's party were hungry, and the whole force stopped to make a meal of roast oxen. McArthur and Cass were only three miles from Detroit with the tantalizing smell of roasting meat in their nostrils.

Captain Snelling, the fire-breathing regular, was also outside the defense perimeter of Detroit. He had won a reluctant consent from General Hull to go to Spring Wells below the fort and watch for the British to cross the river at that most likely spot. Snelling's request to oppose a British landing at

Spring Wells only brought from General Hull orders, which a
regular officer would not deny, to return to Detroit before
dawn of Sunday, 16 August.

So Snelling was not at the Wells when Tecumseh and his
Indians landed there. At sun-up the Indians were on their long
run-walk around the perimeter of Detroit to their ordered
positions around the fort and city. Their canoes littered the
beach when, early in the morning of a fine Sunday, the British
and Canadian brigades came ashore and formed up in the
bridgehead. General Brock was there, his tasseled crimson sash
around his waist. He had little to do but watch the orderly
unfolding of his plans. He heard his cannon from the Sandwich
shore and heard the fleet begin their bombardment on
schedule. Originally, General Brock had reasoned that the
British cannonading would bring General Hull out of the fort
and town to meet him head on in pitched battle. But on
hearing from spies that Cass and McArthur were out with five
hundred soldiers, Brock knew that Hull could not attack him
with such a weakened force. Brock's plan, as he turned his
horse's head into a gap in the marching column of infantry,
was to storm Fort Detroit while the Indians attacked the town.
The sound of the guns grew louder and the pace of the
marching troops quickened. The officers and the sergeants
were shouting to hold the head of column down so the rear
could keep up. British scouts had located the outposts of
Findlay's regiment, deployed west of the fort. A safe distance
in front of the outposts Brock halted the brigades and ordered
the men to eat their cold rations. With his aides trailing behind
him, Brock went forward to make his reconnaissance and final
estimates.

Hull's Sunday began with the renewal of the British bombardment, which had not ended until midnight the night before. Hull was in the fort with the regulars when the first shells landed. It was at once obvious that the prime target of the day was the fort itself. One of the first shells to fall in the fort killed an ensign and one of the paroled gunners from Mackinac Island. The rest of the regulars, men of the 1st and 4th Regiments, took shelter in the casements or around the guns they were assigned to serve on the open bastions and curtain wall. Those who chanced a look through the riverside embrasures could see, and shouted to the others, that the American counter battery fire was falling fair among the British batteries afloat and ashore. A British shell exploded in the yard of the fort. Dr. Hosea Blood, surgeon of the 4th, was severely wounded and was hastily carried into the quarters, where Colonel Miller lay sick and hurt from the old fall from his horse at Maguaga. Two more Americans lay dead in the dusty yard. One was another army doctor, an Ohio man; the other was the unfortunate Lieutenant Hanks, who, as a parole, had been permitted to help the wounded.

Of the four colonels, only Findlay was there to aid the general. He was with his regiment, facing Brock. General Hull was alone in his office, listening to the shells strike and hearing reports from the perimeter. The reports were alarming. The Indians had come. They had come out of the woods and across the fields to the north. They were in among the barns and sheds and outlying houses, moving closer to the stockaded walls of the town. They were threatening the root cellar, where the women and children of the garrison were in shelter. Hull's own family was there. Before ten o'clock a messenger came to headquarters with the news that the Michigan militia, mostly Frenchmen, had deserted its post. Some, the messenger said, had gone over to the Indians. For two days not a word had been heard from McArthur or Cass. They might or might not be coming back to Detroit with Captain Brush's men and the supplies. They were too late. Major General William Hull, all alone, made up his mind. He sent an order to the artillery commander to stop the American battery fire. He sent his son and aide, Captain Abraham Hull, to hoist a clean white table-cloth to ask an armistice and parley. Captain Hull, who had a tendency to do the wrong thing, hurried importantly to the main flagstaff where the stars and stripes hung high over the fort. The general's son with the white cloth clutched under his arm was preparing to bring down his country's flag and run up the white flag of surrender when he was stopped and it was patiently explained that his father's intent was a parley, for which the white cloth must be displayed on a bastion, not on the flagstaff. Only minutes later the white flag was up and the cannon fire eased off and stopped. All was quiet, too, where Findlay's men faced Brock's Canadians and British. Where the Indians were some out-buildings were burning, but there, too, a hush had fallen, as Tecumseh held back the nations.

Hull's parley, called for at ten o'clock in the morning, led, with the speed of a swooping hawk on a cowering rabbit, to the surrender of Detroit at noon. All was lost in the American hutch. The guns on the wall, the supplies in the stores, and all the regular soldiers had gone into captivity. All the militia were put on parole, and General Hull had listed McArthur and Cass in the surrender, as well as Captain Brush, still waiting with the supplies at Frenchtown on the River Raisin. The newly rebuilt brig *Adams* went onto the pile of British booty, along with all the forts from Detroit to and including those at the Maumee Rapids. The collapse and defeat of General and Governor William Hull was complete. Army, territory, honor, all were gone. All that was left to the old man were the women and children of his family and those of other families whom his self-abasement had saved from rape, torture, slavery, and death at the hands of unbridled Indians.

British troops lowered the stars and stripes from the main staff in Fort Detroit, and British troops hoisted the Union Jack on the same pole. Guns were fired in salute and a band played brightly in the fine August afternoon. General Brock and Tecumseh had dismounted and stood together, as they had when they met only two days before. They stood in the presence of the soldiers, red and white. Carefully, in full ceremony, Isaac Brock unclasped the crimson sash from around his waist and gave it to his Indian ally. As solemnly, Tecumseh removed his bead belt, the one with arrows in the design, and gave it to Brock, who tied it around his scarlet uniform coat. Tecumseh's and Brock's days together were very few. They were about to part, Tecumseh for the Northwest, Brock for another battlefield in the east. He wore the Indian's belt of beads and was wearing it two months later when he died, killed in battle at Queenstown Heights. Tecumseh did not wear Brock's sash. It was enough that, in the early hours of 14 August, he had recognized Brock, the man.

XVII

A Second Northwest Army

The garrison at Fort Dearborn on the Chicago River, and the trading settlement on the opposite bank, were very much a family affair in the summer of 1812. Captain Nathan Heald, 1st U.S. Infantry, commanded at the fort. His wife, Rebecca, was the niece of Captain Wells, the Indian Affairs sub-agent and interpreter. The daughter of John Kinzie, the Factor, had married Lieutenant Linai T. Helm, a Kentuckian, across the river. Ensign George Noonan was a graduate of the Military Academy in 1811 and was still unmarried. The other Kinzie children were too young for the ensign. However, the Burns and Ouilmette families, had lived on the south branch of the river, and after the Lee family had been murdered by Winnebago Indians in April 1812, all the white people had gathered close to the fort.

Captain Heald believed that he commanded a safe and secure post. He believed himself to be on good, friendly terms with the Indians in their town upriver. Kinzie carried on his trading. That no supplies came the normal boat route from

Detroit by way of Lieutenant Hanks's post on Mackinac Island was not alarming. The news that Canada and the United States were at war reached Fort Dearborn overland on 10 July and explained the post's isolation that spring and early summer. With fifty-four good soldiers of the 1st, good officers, good sergeants, and enough civilian men, Captain Heald was confident that he could stand off any Indian raid that might come as a result of the war and the general Indian unrest since the 4th Regiment's battle at Tippecanoe.

All was quiet and wary at Fort Dearborn until Winnemeg, called the Catfish, a friendly Potawatomi, arrived on 7 August with serious news and orders from General William Hull. The Americans had invaded Canada, but Mackinac had fallen to the British and the Upper Lakes were endangered. General Hull's orders to Captain Heald were explicit. He was to distribute all the government stores to the Indians. He was to evacuate all the Americans, men, women, and children, whom he would bring overland either to Fort Wayne or to Detroit. The Catfish urged Heald to disregard the order and to stay and hold the fort. On his journey from Detroit the Catfish had been overtaken by the news that Hull had retreated from Canada and that signs of American weakness were bringing out the nations' warriors. The road to Fort Wayne would be dangerous.

Captain Heald was five days preparing to carry out his orders from the general. On 12 August the captain had a farewell council with his Indians. He promised them that on the morrow he would distribute the stores and the arms. Though he spoke in open friendship, loaded cannons looked down from the fort, their cold eyes round and menacing. Black Partridge, rising from his place, stepped up to Captain Heald and gave back the American medal hanging around his neck.

The day of the giving away of stores was cool for August. The Indians noticed that the promised arms were not given out, nor was there liquor or powder among the stores to be distributed. In the quiet of the night of 13 August, Heald had thrown all the powder and whisky down the fort well. The extra guns were broken, their pieces dropped into the river.

On 14 August, Captain Wells came in from Fort Wayne with fifty Miami Indians, supposedly friendly to the Americans. Red Belt, too, arrived that day, the last before the evacuation. Red Belt, a Potawatomi, had been with Tecumseh, and he boasted to Black Partridge of Tecumseh's victory at Brownstown, and of the Americans being stopped at Maguaga, and of the rallying of the far northern nations after Mackinac. Black Partridge's people were stirring. There were some four hundred Indian men, mostly Potawatomi, on the Chicago River that last day. Most of them left the Indian town that night.

By mid-morning on 15 August Fort Dearborn and the civilian town opposite were evacuated. The fort gate stood wide. A shed door across the river swung on its leather hinges in the light breeze off the lake. It banged dully against the log lintel. The dead 'march beat of the drum to which the troops had marched out was silent. The drummer had slung his drum and was settling into the long march out of Illinois across Indiana to Fort Wayne. Two miles south of Fort Dearborn the road led through the sand hills, where the walking would not be easy.

Captain Wells, with the Miami, led the exodus into the sand

hills. When the Potawatomi came running and galloping over the crest the Miami ran. The white people, men and women, braced themselves for the onslaught, ready to fight. Wells, his face blackened with powder, galloped back toward the developing melee. He saw an Indian on a wagon methodically tomahawk the twelve younger children. He saw an Indian he knew and taunted him for fighting like a squaw. They locked in combat, and Wells, raging, went down dead. Lieutenant Helm did not see his wife fought over by two Indians, nor did he see the victor drag her off to the lake and force her under water. Everyone saw Sergeant Holt's wife mounted and laying about her with her husband's sword. Mrs. Heald was fighting with a rifle. She dropped it to bargain with an Indian—a mule and two bottles of whisky for Mrs. Kinzie. The Indian was astride Mrs. Kinzie's back, trying to scalp the struggling woman. At some point in the fight the soldiers charged. Ensign Noonan died with twenty-five of the fifty-four regulars. All twelve of the militiamen were killed. Captain Heald had found the Chief, Black Bird, and was shouting and begging the Indian to call off the killing and make peace. It was done. The Indians drew off to examine their loot and watch from the slopes of the hills.

The Americans found the body of Mrs. Holt, "The Brave Woman," and that of Mrs. Corbord, a soldier's wife, cut to pieces in her struggle. The children lay by the wagon. When they looked for Surgeon Van Voorhees to tend the wounds of the living they found the doctor among the dead. Lieutenant Helm, looking frantically for his wife, saw her, dripping wet, stumbling and running back from the lake shore. Black Partridge, he who had given back his American medal to Captain Heald, had won her in the fight. He had rushed her to the water and there simulated her drowning until the danger passed.

Under the surrender granted by Black Bird, Captain Heald buried his dead and, leading the survivors, returned to the settlement on the Chicago River. On the next day he watched from across the river as Fort Dearborn was burned to ashes. Some of the American prisoners were still there in the unburned houses of the civilians when Captain Charles Roberts came from General Brock to effect a peaceful surrender of Fort Dearborn. He was too late to do anything but make an arrangement with the individual Indians for the ransom of their captives.

No white man, following the defeat of Hull's army in August, could have kept the Indians of the Northwest from rising against the Americans. The one red man who might have kept the peace had died in July, at the age of sixty-five. Little Turtle was buried at Fort Wayne, respected by both Indians and Americans. Without the old Miami chief, the council called at Piqua for 15 August was doomed to failure. Only a few Shawnee and Delaware accepted the United States' invitation, but they soon went home, on hearing of the fall of Detroit and the success of their Potawatomi brothers at the sand hills by the Chicago. Even those meek Indians who came to Piqua went away dissatisfied with the poor gifts the Americans had to offer. The British had been more generous to Tecumseh and those who followed him. Now it was said by those who came from the north that the British Colonel Procter was coming up the Maumee to help the Indians attack

Fort Wayne. It was also said that Colonel Procter paid money for any Yankee scalp.

All over the Northwest young Indians of all the nations were rising. Isolated farms fell to gathering war parties, and, on 3 September, a big scalping party hit the Pigeon Roost settlement in southern Indiana. Two men hunting a bee tree were the first killed. During the evening of that day the raiders scalped another man, five women, and sixteen children. The Pigeon Roost party was a deliberate diversion, for the Indians planned to attack Fort Wayne and Fort Harrison. Captain James Rhea, who had come west with General Harmar's Levies and took his fortune with the army, commanded the seventy-man garrison at Fort Wayne. The first Indian attack came on the night of 6 September. Rhea and his men of the 1st Infantry beat it off. For six days the fort withstood attacks of threat, guile, and by storming. On the evening of 12 September an American relief force arrived at the gates of Fort Wayne, and Rhea let them march in to salute the brave defenders. The Indians had fled; the British had not come.

The initial attack on Fort Harrison on the night of 4 September was more successful. Captain Zachary Taylor of the 7th Infantry was sick that night, as were most of the fifty men he had to defend the fort. The cry of "Fire" woke him before midnight, and he struggled up out of his fever to command. Indians had set fire to a blockhouse on a key corner and were attacking the six-man guard. Taylor was out in the parade, and sick men of the garrison were running and stumbling in the flame glow around him. They fought, all of them, during the night. They fought the uncounted horde of

Indians, and they fought the flames by tipping the burning roof off over the wall. Later that night, when the Indians had given over their attack and the fire had smoldered out, the soldiers of the 7th sealed the gap burned in the wall and the following night they repaired it with logs kept in the fort. For ten more nights and eleven days, Zachary Taylor held his fort against the Indians who were all around it. On the night of 13 September a messenger slipped out of the beleaguered fort, and with a companion crept through the tight ring of Indians. Three days later a relief force came to Fort Harrison. They found the garrison exhausted by their long effort and many still sick with the fever. In the fort were three new graves and there were three wounded men in the hospital. Young Captain Taylor, more gaunt than ever after his ordeal, was awarded the brevet rank of major (the first brevet in the U.S. army), for his tenacity, his leadership, and his courage.

Behind the big war parties was the guiding hand of Tecumseh, encouraged by Colonel Procter and the British government. The big raids, and the lesser, too, that ignited fires of fear and anger across the American Northwest as far as the Mississippi were intended by the British to keep the Second Western Army from counterattacking. This other American army was the result of a cry from General Hull for reinforcement at Detroit. Brigadier James Winchester was appointed to command the reinforcements for Hull, and this second army, too late to save Hull, found the men to save the forts Wayne and Harrison. Colonel William Russell, the U.S. Ranger, en route through Vincennes, found units of the new army there which he used to relieve Taylor. William Henry Harrison was near Piqua with Winchester's main force when

Fort Wayne was attacked. He was able to dispatch fast-moving units to the aid of that fort.

Governor Harrison's position in command of General Winchester's troops in August, and his presence with them, was irregular. Harrison was there because he was too popular in the American Northwest to be left out and too able an officer to be ignored. Washington City, in its remote wisdom, created James Winchester a Brigadier General in March 1812. The new general's previous military service had ended twenty-nine years before, when he had been a captain of Maryland Continentals. His residence and presence at his home in Tennessee in the summer of 1812 made him the logical choice to raise and command the new army. At the age of sixty, General Winchester found arduous the work of recruiting and training a new regiment of U.S. Infantry, the 17th, and one thousand wild Kentuckians, who were to be his relief force. The Kentuckians gave the old veteran particular trouble. Although a resident of the west for many years, James Winchester had never discarded his eastern ideas and still clothed his attitude in the polite garb of his native Maryland. William Henry Harrison, among the rabble of the west, was still a Harrison of Berkeley Hundred, and therefore was reliable and a gentleman. While General Winchester was busying himself with important organizational matters in Kentucky, he permitted Harrison to command his troops, who were gathering in the rough camp in Ohio.

Beside being "The General" to all men of the west, William Henry Harrison had virtually three general's commissions in his field desk. As governor of Indiana he was commander in chief of that Territory's militia. Governor Scott of Kentucky, on the request of his successor, Isaac Shelby, and with the enthusiastic consent of the state's Council, had made the governor of Indiana a major general of the Kentucky militia. It was an appointment neither tendered nor accepted as honorary. Finally, on 22 August 1812, Secretary of War Eustis proffered Harrison a brigadier general's commission in the U.S. army, under orders to conduct offensive action in Indiana and Illinois. Harrison did not accept the federal commission at once. If he did, he would be forever junior in rank to the unrespected Winchester. On the other hand, all his brother governors, from Meigs of Ohio to Ninian Edwards of Illinois to Benjamin Howard in distant Missouri, counted on him for leadership in the war against the British in Canada. While yet of two minds about the U.S. commission, Harrison acted like a general in command, and he moved boldly with Winchester's men northward toward the Maumee, in aid of Fort Wayne.

The Second Western Army was big and growing bigger as the crackling of Indian raids was heard through all the Northwest. By September some seven thousand Kentucky men were taking up their arms in defense or offense. The Ohioans were alert. Two thousand Pennsylvanians and fifteen hundred Virginians were moving into Ohio to stiffen the guard and, for extra pay, to build roads of access to the southern shore of Lake Erie. Mounted riflemen from Kentucky were in western Indiana keeping back the nations in wild Illinois. Five hundred more of these special mounted men were with Harrison, and their colonel, the Honorable Richard M. Johnson, rode close to the three-times general. The old 1st Regiment, broken now with its losses at Detroit and at Dearborn, maintained the small forts from Fort Wayne in Miami country to Fort Madison in the country of the fierce Winnebago. The new 17th Infantry was learning the drill as their colonel, Samuel Wells, had observed it and learned it from General Harrison on the Tippecanoe campaign.

Winchester's deputy commander had twenty-one hundred men at Cincinnati when he moved north to Piqua. Four more regiments were on the way to join him, as were guns requisitioned from Pittsburgh. He moved quickly, without orders or authority, to the relief of Fort Wayne, and he himself was there on 12 September. While he waited the coming of General Winchester, Harrison tidied up the land around the fort. Strong detachments rode out to punish the Indians who had broken their trust to the United States. Towns were burned, storehouses destroyed, and the detachments rode back, splashing through the headwaters of many rivers, to where their General Harrison held safe once more the key fort named for "Mad Anthony Wayne."

XVIII

A New Army, A New Navy

In pomp and with all his comforts, Brigadier General James Winchester arrived at Fort Wayne on 18 September to assume command of his army. Politely, and in keeping with his word, William Henry Harrison turned over the troops who adored him to the veteran of the Revolution. Harrison was a major general of Kentucky that day. He had not yet accepted the U.S. commission and was quite conscious of the frontier fact, supported by the other western governors, that the state rank of a major general outranked that of a U.S. Brigadier General. Harrison was able to emphasize this fact in taking with him on his departure Johnson's fine mounted men and another Kentucky rifle unit. With these and other state units he planned to strike at the Illinois River settlements where even the crazy old Shawnee Prophet with his beads was being given credence. Before they would let their hero go, the men of Winchester's army heard Harrison lecture them on discipline, and duty, and loyalty. The men were reconciled to their new general through the hope that Old Tippecanoe would return to lead them again.

Harrison was back even sooner than he expected. As seniority and authority confused the command structure of the Northwest's First Army and threatened the Second Army, so, too, was Washington City confused. The whole war, as President Madison saw it, as the Secretaries of War, Navy, and State directed it, and as Congress sought to control it, was flying off in all directions as if spun on a wheel of chance.

The few frigates of the U.S. navy, hull down over the off-shore horizon, were fighting British ships in gallant engagements that won their captains fame and heartened the civilian population, but did not win the war and scarcely dented the oaken walls of the British navy. Federalist New England remained doggedly loyal in its dissent while maintaining militia guards along the New Brunswick–Maine border. These guards fraternized pleasantly with the Canadian guards across the bridge. At the other extremity of the United States, the people of Tennessee and a red-headed general with local rank were eyeing the belligerent Indians in Alabama and Mississippi and the Spanish-French city of New Orleans. Old General Hull, the villain and dastard of 1812, was being condemned to death on horrible charges. General Dearborn's Northern Army had done nothing. The Niagara wing had made no commitment to attack during the long summer. General Brock, back from his Detroit victory, was forcing American action on the Niagara for the autumn. On Lake Ontario and Lake Champlain, the United States navy was making the beginnings of battle fleets while the army stood by and waited. In the

Northeast, from the Niagara land bridge to the Canadian border on Lake Champlain, a local truce existed. In the interests of peace, the governor general had shared with General Dearborn his foreknowledge of the rescinding of the Orders in Council and had proposed a truce. Dearborn, as anxious as Prevost to buy time to prepare for a war for which both were unprepared, agreed to the truce. With the War Hawks nudging him to further efforts, President Madison finally ended the truce on 8 September. Issues other than the Orders in Council held the attention of the diplomats, who, quite apart from the army and navy, were waging their own war with Great Britain.

In a government confused with the conduct of five simultaneous wars in 1812, each responsible department in Washington City seemed to multiply the general confusion. President Madison, with his Secretary of War, had condemned the field armies to stagnation by appointing old worn-out generals, all Revolutionary War veterans, as their commanders. In the first year of the war with Britain, the bright young soldiers had not risen out of the slough of inaction to challenge the venerable old heroes of time-wilted glory. William Henry Harrison was the first of the new soldiers to emerge and to attain the bright stars of general's rank.

Harrison's success at Tippecanoe, although providing a firm base for the future, had not been enough. The command went to Hull. Neither was the coalition of western governors enough to win Harrison the command of the Second Northwest Army that went to Winchester. But the confidence of his fellow governors, aided by the dynamism of Henry Clay, leader of the congressional War Hawks, won for Harrison a commission in the west. Faced with the necessity of appointing a supreme commander in the west, President Mac son offered the post to his Secretary of State, James Monroe. The tall, blue-eyed Secretary of State, with a scar on his shoulder from a wound taken in the Battle of Trenton in 1776, declined the honor, as a risk to a distinguished and rising political career. Governor William Henry Harrison was the President's second choice to "Command the Northwest Army."

The commission, which the thirty-nine-year-old governor of Indiana accepted, gave him command over General Winchester's relief army. Harrison's orders gave him command of all the regulars in the west, as well as of the volunteers and militia of Ohio, Indiana, Virginia, and Kentucky. Artillery from the Pittsburgh arsenal was promised him, and the control of funds was granted through the commissioner in Kentucky. Harrison's orders were to defend the frontier, retake Detroit, and attack Canada, and to "exercise your own discretion, and act in all cases according to your own discretion." Every man in the west, from Governor Shelby's "Board of War" to the meanest private of the most obscure militia company, hailed with cheers of hope Harrison's appointment as virtual dictator of war in the Northwest.

Harrison received his commission and his orders at Piqua on 24 September, after he had returned the relief army to General Winchester's command. With the grace and tact of leadership, General Harrison left Winchester the command of his force and assigned it the active role in the immediate execution of Harrison's over-all plan of campaign. Winchester was to continue his sweep down the Maumee to probe and contain the enemy along that line of march to the lost city of Detroit.

Two other columns would converge on the Maumee Rapids for the march around the western end of Lake Erie into Michigan and on into Canada. The second column was to be a secure and developed supply route along the old fort line stabbing upward through western Ohio. The easternmost force from Pittsburgh would build roads and forts to Sandusky on Lake Erie to bring the artillery train to the army on the lower Maumee. By the spring of 1813 General Harrison would be ready to reconquer the lost territory and to conquer new lands.

Buried in the instructive letters and dispatches from Washington City was one which underscored every hope of the campaign's success: the navy would build a battle fleet on Lake Erie. Commodore Isaac Chauncey had been given naval command on Lake Ontario, and he, in turn, was ordered to detach an officer to create a navy on the upper lakes. Lieutenant Jesse Elliott, U.S.N., twenty-seven years old, arrived at Buffalo on 8 October 1812, a sailor pauper, a commodore without a ship, a young man with only ambition. But opportunity arrived the same day, at the British anchorage at Fort Erie, across the water from Buffalo. On 8 October the Northwest Company's armed brig *Caledonia*, in from Detroit with a hold full of rich furs, dropped anchor under the guns of the fort and the downriver batteries. With her was the prize *Adams*, taken by the British at Detroit and renamed for that city. From the high view from Black Rock Jesse Elliott could also see two fine vessels, riding bows into the swift current. Elliott wanted those two brigs for his fleet. That night he got them.

Elliot, with only fifty unarmed sailors, was poor in men for the cutting-out expedition he had in mind. But he was fortunate. Colonel Winfield Scott was at Buffalo, and he was eager to lend the navy lieutenant arms and soldiers for the adventure. The party, armed impromptu with swords, cutlasses, pistols, and pikes, set out in two boats in the dark of midnight. For three hours they battled the current rushing into the funnel of the river. Elliott lay his boat alongside *Detroit* unobserved as the watch was tolling six bells. With a volley of muskets, the fifty men went over the sides of the brig. *Caledonia* came under attack two minutes later, and within five minutes Sailing Master George Watts and Captain Nathan Towsom of the artillery were aboard and in command of *Caledonia.* Within ten minutes of boarding, both prizes, top sails sheeted home, were standing out from the Canadian shore. The capture had been easy, but the journey home was hard. The way led under the guns of Fort Erie and the two downriver batteries. Speed was necessary, but the wind was light and the current strong, and the British guns followed the two captured vessels all along their way. For many long minutes of cannonading, *Detroit,* her own guns in action, drifted helplessly with the shove of the current. Then, with a shudder and a grinding, she went ashore on Squaw Island. There, close to the American shore, she lay heeled over to port, stranded, her guns canted and silent. *Caledonia* was more fortunate. She got in behind the island and grounded gently on the safe American shore. Working in the dark, Elliott hustled his forty-six prisoners ashore and with his own men removed the stores which were the booty from Hull's defeat. The British, hard stung and angry as hornets, mounted an attack on the stranded *Detroit.* Coming out of the dark and noise of the wild night they took her. Colonel Winfield Scott, at the very beginning of a great career, led an army force, with all others who would come, and took her back again. The new day was dawning and the American flag flew above the British at the canted masthead. All day the Americans worked under the fire of the British long guns to patch and refloat the stranded brig. But, toward evening, the British brought up *Lady Prevost* to support with her broadside a new British attempt to retake their prize. Knowing he could not save her now, Lieutenant Elliott gave the order to burn *Detroit.* And so, in smoke and flame, the short life of *Adams* ended at the hands of the Americans who had built her.

The British had two warships less and Elliott had a one-ship navy. *Caledonia* was the white-winged fledgling of the Lake Erie fleet, but there was hope and promise of others. Westward, down the coast where the horn of Pennsylvania thrusts up to the Erie shore, behind the headland and the sandbars of Presque Isle, the American Navy Department was building a nest to cradle five ships of war: two brigs and three schooner-rigged big-gun boats. Presque Isle was a sheltered place, a quiet place, to raise the ribs and plank the hulls and cut the spars. It was accessible by river and portage to the stores at Pittsburgh. While *Caledonia* waited, safe under the American guns, the vessels were building at Presque Isle and William Henry Harrison's army was gathering and fighting far up the fresh water.

XIX

Autumn Armies

Ships being built in the haven of an eastern Lake Erie harbor were remote from the five army scouts and the seven "friendly" Indians who had joined them in a camp by a small brook trickling its way toward the lake. The ships were complex things of wood and canvas and cordage and iron, cunningly contrived into great engines of war. The men by the brook were the simplest basic tool of man's intent for war. That night, as the scouts slept, the "friendly" Indians killed them. Their scalped, plundered, and corrupted bodies were found by their army friends who were sent out to search for them.

Colonel Russell, with three small companies of U.S. Rangers, joined Governor Edwards of Illinois and a body of mounted militia a little north and west of Vincennes. The force of three hundred and sixty men was to meet a much larger force for a reprisal raid against the Kickapoo towns, whose warriors were held culpable for the Fort Dearborn raid. When the larger force did not arrive at the rendezvous, Russell and Edwards, marching fast and traveling light, struck out for the Indian town at the north end of Peoria Lake, a broad stretch of the Illinois River. They hit the town hard, and the Indians fled. The Americans, in pursuit, followed into the swamp and across the river. The scattered encounters were man to man and hand to hand, with the white man everywhere the victor. At the now empty village soldiers burned the huts and harvest-full corn stores, while Edwards's mounted men rounded up the eighty horses of the Indians' herd. Before they quit the burning village, Colonel Russell sent men into the woods and fields and swamps, and even across the river, to gather in the bodies of slain Indians. They found twenty, brought them back, and left them, neatly arranged in a row, for those returning to find and take warning.

The massacre at the Peoria Lake village was in October of 1812. This and the brookside slaughter of the five scouts marked the beginning of the autumn war waged by William Henry Harrison. Reprisal raids by substantial white forces were launched from rendezvous called for convenient places throughout the Northwest. Brigadier General Samuel Hopkins of Kentucky, whose large force of half-hearted volunteers had not kept the rendezvous with Russell, tried again in November, this time with regulars under Brevet Major Zachary Taylor with his massed Kentucky militia. Their target was the rebuilt Prophet's Town, their purpose to draw back onto home defense independent Indians who had rallied to their old leader, Tecumseh, now to all intents and purposes a brigadier general in the British camp. They burned the forty empty houses they found in the town, fought and lost sixteen killed to the Indians found hiding in the woods, and marched back again to Fort Harrison through the first heavy snowfall of winter.

Whatever the specific intent that guided each individual raiding force, the purpose of Harrison's autumn campaign was to restore the Indian nations to their former neutrality under the Council of Greenville and subsequent treaties. Without safe passage over the open roads through the Indian lands in Ohio and Indiana, the army on the lower Maumee could not be supplied for the liberation of Michigan or the invasion of Canada. Of all the autumn raids, that of Lieutenant Colonel John Campbell did most to achieve the general's purpose.

The lieutenant colonel commanding the new 18th Infantry was given his orders at Franklin, Ohio, on 25 November. Campbell was given a six-hundred-man force to defeat or disperse a large gathering of Miami on the Mississinewa River, a gathering whose peaceful intent was suspect. If Campbell's orders were clear and simple, his instructions were complex. While he was to attack the Miami with ruthless force, he was urged to spare the lives of a long list of friendly Miami leaders. Richardville, the second chief of the nation, led the list, which included Silver Heels, White Lion, Pecan, Charley of the Eel River Miami, Old Godfroy and his wife, and, of course, the son and the brother of Little Turtle. To further hamper the direct approach of a soldier to his work, Colonel Campbell was to march around the Delaware towns, lest his soldiers disturb the precarious peace of that nation.

The force moved quickly to Dayton, where it had to wait for a pack train for the infantry, the 19th, and two small regiments of Pennsylvanians, one a regiment of good riflemen, the other the proud Pittsburgh Blues. The weather was cold when Campbell left Greenville on 14 December for Silver

Heels' town on the Mississinewa. The hooves of his horse clopped loudly on the frozen ground as Major James V. Ball, at the head of his cavalry, turned into the road to the west. Major Ball had been a horse soldier since the days of Wayne's Legion. Now he commanded a squadron of helmeted troopers of the 2nd Light Dragoons. Behind his regulars the easy riders of Lieutenant Colonel James Simrall's Kentucky Dragoons took to the road, forage bags heavy with corn behind their saddles.

The third day's march covered forty miles, and the troopers arrived, unexpected, at the first Indian town. They killed eight warriors there and captured eight more, along with many women and children. They left the town black ashes in the snow, the cattle dead lumps on the white fields. Then, taking only the mounted men, Campbell pushed on the two miles to Silver Heels' town. It had been hastily abandoned. By the time the infantry came up, the town was destroyed. The force made a fortified camp on the bank of the Mississinewa.

Toward midnight, sentries reported to Major Ball, the field officer on duty, that Indians were about. He doubled the guard. At four in the morning on 18 December the adjutant called a conference of field officers at the colonel's fire. The whole camp was alert, each man standing to, with his blanket draped around his shoulders, shifting his weight from one cold foot to the other. The senior officers were still huddled close to the warmth of the fire when the Indians attacked. They struck the angle where the Light Dragoons joined Simrall's men. Captain Pierce of Kentucky was shot as he and his men recoiled under the fierce attack. When the Pittsburgh Blues charged and restored the position, they found the captain dead and scalped. For an hour the whole camp fought, while Campbell disengaged three troops of Kentucky Dragoons to mount and rally. Behind a concentrated fire by the Pittsburgh men, the cavalry charged and drove the Indians away. The battle was over by sun-up of the cold morning. The fifteen Indian dead were all young men of Silver Heels' band, and the prisoners taken told Campbell that Little Thunder, a nephew of Little Turtle, had been one of their leaders in the attack. They also confirmed to the colonel that Tecumseh and a big war party were further down the Mississinewa, ready to come up.

Carrying forty-two wounded, and eight dead and beyond pain, Colonel Campbell withdrew. For seventeen of the wounded, slung in litters, the journey back through the aching cold was torture. The rest plodded wearily through the snow on scant rations until a relief appeared on the road ahead, shouting a welcome and waving loaves of good oven-baked bread. Tecumseh had not followed. The expedition was back, and though half the six hundred were lost to service with frostbite, Campbell had achieved his mission. The friendly Miami chiefs reasserted their control and cooled the ardor of the young warriors. The most recalcitrant of the young men went off with Little Thunder to join Tecumseh, leaving the rest to an adequate semblance of the old neutrality. Tecumseh himself, who had been agitating and recruiting in the Northwest, turned his personal attention to the lower Maumee, where his British friends had been anxiously watching Winchester's slow descent of that river.

Brigadier General James Winchester was having his troubles with his command, troubles such as only an aloof and haughty commander can have. He began his march from Fort Wayne on 22 September, three days after taking back the command from Harrison. The change-over in commanders had disorganized the army. Winchester's slow, ponderous movement down the north bank of the Maumee improved the morale neither of the eager soldiers nor of the reluctant ones. The army encountered Indians, and when the bodies of the five scouts were found beside the brook, Winchester hurriedly formed a tight defensive camp. He was still twenty miles from his first objective, Fort Defiance. What Winchester did not know, as he rolled down the river like a boulder in a freshet, was that he was on a collision course with a British force. Major Muir, with two hundred and fifty regulars and militiamen, and a battery of field guns, was moving upriver behind a screen of eight hundred Indians to attack Fort Wayne. The major had already passed Fort Defiance. Of Winchester's scouts only a Sergeant McCoy had pierced the screen of the Britisher's Indians, and he was now a bound prisoner. But McCoy was a convincing liar as he described to Major Muir the size and strength of the American army. Muir fell back, and when his Indians showed their petulance by deserting, the British commander could do nothing but re-embark his guns and retreat to below the rapids. Made aware at last of what lay ahead, General Winchester continued his march even more slowly, even more cautiously. At the old camp ground, near the rotting walls of Anthony Wayne's old Fort Defiance, he camped again. In his well-guarded tent Winchester wrote to Harrison, telling of his peril in the face of a British army downriver. In the camp outside the general's compound the men were hungry and cold. Neither the promised food nor the expected winter clothing had come. In the crisp autumn nights patience wore thin, discipline crumbled. One regiment was near to open mutiny.

General Harrison was at St. Marys, near Fort Wayne, with three thousand troops when he heard that Winchester had encountered British regulars. Delaying only long enough to issue three days' rations, Harrison took one thousand mounted riflemen, assembled to be used on an aborted strike for Detroit via the St. Joseph River, and set out to reinforce Winchester and his army. Marching through a pelting rain, the horsemen overtook the supply column, which had been stalled by Indians. Sleeping that night in the wet cold leaves, Harrison's men and the supply column were up early and away. They swept through the dripping forest in five long columns, their leaders hallooing like huntsmen on a deer drive. Impatient and anxious, General Harrison spurred on ahead. He arrived quietly and unnoticed at Winchester's camp at dusk. From Brigadier General James Winchester, who had so recently been his senior in rank, General Harrison learned the state of the army and the panic of its commander. He acted in the morning of 3 October.

Instead of "Reveille," Harrison had the "Alarm" beaten. From a tent he watched the dilatory turnout of the troops. When they were all assembled, General Harrison revealed himself to the parade. In terms that only a strong and loved commander can use he shamed them before themselves. He called them down and he dressed them up until they stood straight in their ranks. He appealed to them as men and soldiers and patriots. When they were ready to cheer he told them of his appointment as their commander in chief. Then they cheered him, three times three, and marched off to their duty, heads high, shoulders back, sergeants shouting. By the afternoon the whole command was working on the new fort, to be named Fort Winchester, that Harrison had ordered built. In the general's tent, with a polite Winchester, Harrison was planning a reconnaissance in force to the Maumee Rapids by the horsemen that came from St. Marys. The foray, though successful, was later to irritate Winchester, but on that day no unbecoming anger marred his hospitality to Harrison. On the morning of 4 October Winchester bade Harrison farewell, as one gentleman to another.

Alone again with his command, which Harrison had restored to him, General Winchester was faced with a supply and stores situation that, as it worsened, would build into a major problem. Winchester's problem was Harrison's, too. Somewhere, somehow, the commander must find, assemble, and send food and warm clothing, particularly warm clothing, to the army on the Maumee. The winter uniforms, which had been ordered for the regulars in good time, had not arrived at Pittsburgh. The militia on the Maumee were without warm shirts from their state and territorial governors. October grew cold, and the wind and rains battered down the red and gold leaves from the autumn trees. Snow came in November, and the bare branches did not stop the force of the chilling winter winds blowing on the soldiers as they huddled around their camp fires. Twice General Winchester moved the camp in search of convenient firewood for the huts that he had permitted the men to build. Now a growing sick list held Winchester from his objective on the lower river.

A breakdown of the contract system that supplied the

soldiers' food plagued Harrison at his headquarters in Franklin, Ohio. The civilian contractors did not fill the depots. In the frosts and thaws of autumn the pack trains and wagons moved slowly to the supply points. Only a trickle got through to the hungry men at the head of the line.

General William Henry Harrison was behind schedule on his winter campaign. He would not have his stockpile of a million rations on the lower Maumee by his jump-off date, set for 20 January 1813. Though the eastern wing of his army was well organized at upper and lower Sandusky, the heavy siege artillery needed to attack Malden was not yet up from Pittsburgh. In his correspondence with Washington City, Harrison was showing his pessimism. He had called off proposed raids on Indian villages. His cavalry was in winter quarters for lack of forage. More and more he was counting on a summer campaign in conjunction with the new fleet, slowly building on the shore of Lake Erie. Still aggressive, however, Harrison on 4 January wrote to James Monroe, then acting as Secretary of War, that he still hoped to make a winter attack on Malden with four thousand men.

In early December Harrison had partially solved Winchester's supply problem. By borrowing from stores intended as gifts to friendly Indians, heavy clothes had reached the army on the Maumee. The women of Kentucky had assembled and sent some eighteen hundred warm shirts to Winchester's men, and uniforms and shoes for Colonel Wells's 17th Infantry, the shock troops for the whole army, had at last reached the soldiers. Finally able to move forward, Winchester, on Harrison's orders, proceeded down the Maumee. At last, after a slow march, looking over his shoulder at every step for

Tecumseh's Indians, Winchester's army arrived below the Maumee Rapids and pitched camp on the left bank, above the old battle ground where Wayne had won his victory. On that spot Winchester would be on the old established supply line used by Hull, and at the end of the new road from Sandusky over a fifteen-mile causeway which was being built across the Black Swamp.

With a good January thaw, supplies moving at last, and Winchester below the Rapids by 10 January, General Harrison was hopeful about launching his winter campaign. So he wrote James Monroe on 15 January 1813 from upper Sandusky. The new date for the beginning of the march from the Maumee had been put over to the first week in February. Winchester had orders not to leave his camp below the Maumee Rapids.

XX

Frenchtown

General Winchester had many rational reasons for disobeying Harrison's orders to stay at the new camp at the Maumee Rapids. The "orders," though detailed, were only implied, and Winchester had received a call for aid from Frenchtown, a call so desperate that no gentleman could fail to give it heed. To the officers summoned to a conference, James Winchester explained the situation in that beset community, half way between the Maumee Rapids and Detroit.

A courier had come with a rumor that the English and Canadians were about to interpose a force at Frenchtown to deny the advancing Americans that important crossing on the road to Detroit. It was further rumored that all the inhabitants who were sympathetic to the American cause would be evacuated to Malden. All the officers knew the hardships to young and aged, to women and children, that such a winter journey entailed. More convincing to the assembly was the travel-stained messenger standing by the general's chair. He was still wearing his traveling cloak, and his words came in gasps as he told of the threat of massacre and destruction promised by Indians who passed that way as they fled before Winchester's army.

There was no question in the minds of the militia officers but that Winchester, and they with him, should go to save Frenchtown. None could conceive that such a humanitarian mission did not supersede General Harrison's orders. Besides, a move now would put Winchester's army thirty miles along the road to Detroit and, tactically, would seize an important river crossing which would have to be fought for if held by the enemy. The messenger from Frenchtown also pointed out that the British intended to take away to Malden a large cache of food. Of the officers at the conference only Colonel Samuel Wells, the regular soldier commanding the 17th Infantry, was not convinced by the arguments for going at once to Frenchtown. Such a headlong rescue expedition did not take into consideration General Harrison's campaign as a whole. General Winchester called for a vote, and Colonel Wells was overruled.

Without delay the first contingent of the mercy expedition, five hundred and fifty men, set out on the morning of 17 January 1813. Lieutenant Colonel William Lewis led the force. A few hours later Lieutenant Colonel John Allen followed with one hundred and ten Kentuckians. The two forces combined at Maumee Bay, where they bivouacked for the night. To avoid the worst of the snowdrifts that had hampered the march to the Rapids and to Maumee Bay, the two colonels intended to march over the marginal ice that covered the Lake Erie shore. General Winchester sat down to write and tell General Harrison that he was away with the

army to the River Raisin. He was able to add a postscript to the
letter before it was sent. Winchester had just heard that there
were four hundred Indians at the Raisin and that Colonel
Elliott was expected momentarily with troops from Malden.
Blandly, the general of the army's left wing told his commanding officer that he, General Harrison, probably would
have to send the right wing to co-operate with the left.
General Winchester saw the messenger off on the sixty-five-
mile winter journey to Harrison at upper Sandusky or King
Crane's Town. Before Winchester could receive a reply he
would be almost one hundred miles away.

Moving rapidly in the cold of early morning, Colonel Lewis
arrived near mid-day on the south side of the River Raisin.
Across the ice lay Frenchtown, two hundred Canadians of the
Essex militia, a single howitzer, and about four hundred
Indians led by Round Head and the six-foot-tall Wyandot,
Walk-In-The-Water. Colonel Lewis chose to charge. The
American battle line moved slowly across the slippery glare ice
of the river. For that short but tricky crossing they were under
the blaze of enemy musketfire. Once on the north shore, the
pace of the charge picked up, as did its fury. The Canadians
fell back across the small fields, each field surrounded by a low
puncheon fence. Behind each fence and at each house the
Canadians stopped to fire. The Americans continued their
pursuit in rushes, vaulting the fences, plowing through the
drifts, probing cautiously through the houses and through the
barns warmed by the huddled cattle. On the American right,
Major Graves and Major Madison charged for the British
howitzer, but Bombardier Kitson and his crew drew off the
precious piece under covering fire that held the majors and

their men pinned down behind a puncheon fence. Slowly Colonel Lewis's men pushed the enemy back through the settlement, to their last stand at the edge of the wood, two miles north of the river. The early dusk of January drew in and the confronting forces slackened their fire in the failing light. The Canadians and Indians quietly disappeared into the gloom of the woods. The Americans, rifles or muskets canted over their shoulders, trudged slowly back along the beaten paths through the snow to the houses they had charged and set free. The Americans had come a long distance and had had a long day. The fifty-five wounded were warm in the houses. The twelve American dead lay stiff and frozen under blankets in a shed. Around a campfire before a lean-to, a Kentuckian was boasting: an Indian, seeing the company charge, had yelled out "Kentucky, by God," grabbed his musket, and ran. The Kentuckians under their Kentucky colonel had done well.

The next morning Colonel Lewis made fortified camp behind the strongest of the fences and waited the arrival of Winchester, summoned by a night-riding messenger carrying the news of victory. Winchester did not tarry. He called out Colonel Wells and the 17th Infantry, and while he waited for the horses to be harnessed and his sleigh brought up, he wrote a quick note to Harrison telling of Lewis's success. When he finally set out in his sleigh behind a brisk team, General Winchester had divided his forces in two. With the three hundred regulars marching behind his sleigh, he would have about a thousand men of the left wing on the River Raisin. There would be a thousand men holding the camp at the rapids. Confidence, warm as the laprobe over the general's knee, rode forward with the sleigh that afternoon.

The following day, 20 January, Winchester arrived at Frenchtown. He inspected the camp with Lewis and watched as Colonel Wells moved into position by a house and barn on the right of Lewis's position. The American position faced an orchard, a long hollow, and the woods into which the Canadians had disappeared. Satisfied that his army was ready to meet a counterattack, General Winchester got into his sleigh and was driven back across the frozen river to the house of Francis Navarre. There, in the big room where the Frenchman did his trading, Winchester made his headquarters.

All was safe, warm, and comfortable in the large room, where the fire was burning brightly. The nearest troops were half a mile away. The company of his staff was congenial in success, and the citizens of Frenchtown who came to call were grateful for their safety behind the shield of the American soldiers.

On 21 January, more warm clothes were distributed to the Kentucky men behind the puncheon fence. Winchester had brought up some cartridges, too, but these he chose to keep in reserve, though Lewis's men were down to ten rounds each. During the day rumors came to headquarters that the British and their Indians were coming. General Winchester's credulity was exhausted and he chose to follow the advice of the more skeptical of his visitors, refusing to listen to the plea of Colonel Wells to move headquarters nearer to the troops. However, he did give his nervous, anxious, contrary colonel permission to return to the rapids to bring up reinforcements. A militia major named McClanahan commanded the regulars on the right wing in the fields beyond the protection of the fence. By midnight the camp was quiet, the soldiers asleep at last. The sentries, in borrowed coats, kept a changing watch in the bitter cold. Because of the still, windless, bitterness of the night, the compassionate general had not sent out patrols to watch the roads, particularly that one from Detroit and Brownstown across the river ice from Malden. He had, however, called for an early reveille to be beaten well before the winter dawn.

A sentry roused up the drummer boy at Colonel Lewis's headquarters and sent him shivering out into the dark. With cramped fingers the boy clutched the sticks and beat out a ragged "Three Camps." The sleeping men who heard the drum call heard the thump of cannon firing, too, and before they could scramble to their feet three cannister shells burst in the camp, followed by a bursting howitzer bomb. Some had seen the lazy arc of the shell coming from the field in front of the northern wood. The American sentries were firing into the dark beyond the puncheon fence and into the blackness in front of the exposed regulars. Before the British cannon could fire again into the camp, the attacking force struck hard on the regulars from out of the night.

The British Colonel Procter had come across the ice from Malden to Brownstown the day before. With him he had brought Colonel St. George and the 41st Foot, some Royal Newfoundlands, and some men of the 10th Veteran Battalion, all regulars, as well as a marine detachment from the fleet. At Brownstown he had reorganized Major Reynold's Essex militia, whom Lewis had driven away on 18 January. Procter had between six hundred and eight hundred Indians, under Round Head, who were eager to go to Frenchtown again, along with the six hundred white soldiers. With the Indians, keeping up their ardor and co-ordinating their movements, were thirty-two of Colonel Elliott's men, whom the British Indian Department called "interpreters." The coldness of the night did not hold back Procter, his six hundred white men, his Indians, and his battery of three 3-pounders and the howitzer. They marched the snowy road from Brownstown purposefully, like a shambling black bear going to a favorite berry patch. Where the road came out of the woods into the cleared land of the Frenchtown settlement, Procter's force deployed embracing arms to right and left. The regulars took the center, facing the strong puncheon fence behind which Lewis' Kentuckians slept. The Canadian militia and the Indians, groping in the dark, found the American angle to their right and the Yankee regulars in the field to their left. The red men and the white men hunkered down in their places to wait the signal. All was quiet. From in front of the British regulars the cannon roared and the black bear charged.

The 17th Infantry, without a fence for protection or comfort, recoiled. They gathered in a group behind the barn, but when the enemy came again, in the now lightening sky, again they fell back. General Winchester came hurrying up from his headquarters, a gray shadow in the dawn. Colonel Lewis, his own troops at least holding their own behind the fence, came running over to the right wing, a hundred of his Kentuckians at his back. They could not hold the slow retreat of the infantry, nor could the two commanders, now standing together in the confusion. When at last all order collapsed and the men turned and ran, their general and their colonel could do nothing but run with them, scattering through the woods south of the River Raisin. Wide-circling Indians met the fleeing white men in that wood. There a gleeful slaughter took place as the Indians scalped and butchered the hated Kentuckians and the bluecoated soldiers.

Winchester and Lewis had veered off from the running mob. They had slowed to a walk and were crossing a small bridge over a stream when suddenly Round Head himself appeared in front of them. He had a small band with him. The two men were prisoners of the Wyandot chief. Round Head let his warriors strip the two high-ranking Americans to their boots, britches, and shirts, then, prodding them before him, he took them the long way around, to Colonel Procter's command post near the guns.

Behind the puncheon fence the Kentuckians had held off the attack until dawn. With light to see the blade of the foresight in the notch of the rearsight, their slim brown rifles took over their part of the battlefield. From behind the pickets they could keep the infantry at a distance. Procter's light artillery, playing on the fence line, was silenced, too, by the deadly rifles that reached the gunners serving the pieces. Procter was forced to move his guns back out of effective range. About ten o'clock in the morning the two majors who, following the departure of Lewis, had commanded at the fence, gave the Kentuckians permission to eat. Elias Darnell was kneeling by his wounded brother, Allen, helping him to eat. Through a gap in the puncheons he saw a man, British to judge by the coat, coming toward the American line under a flag of truce. Elias was still with his brother when the emissary walked by. Looking up, he saw that the man in the borrowed coat was General Winchester, who silently passed on to where the two majors were waiting to receive him.

Though a prisoner of war, and without authority to command, General Winchester ordered his two former subordinates to surrender, even as he had done. Their ammunition low, their right demolished, the Indians returning from their bloody work in the woods over the river, and assured by Winchester of Procter's honorable and generous terms, the majors acceded to their general's illegal order. Hesitantly, reluctantly, the Kentuckians rose up from behind their fence. Elliott's Indians were back, plundering among the houses, drawing closer to where those Kentuckians still under arms stood anxiously over their wounded lying beside the fence. The majors would not move, and Procter himself was summoned. Reluctantly, Colonel Procter furnished a British guard for the prisoners to protect them. He also promised that a guard would be set over the wounded and that sleds would be sent from Malden to fetch them. Assured by a British officer's word, the prisoners marched off, the British and the Canadians with them. Elias Darnell stayed with his brother. Major Reynolds of the Essex militia came in with three interpreters. These, Darnell learned, were the promised guard for the American wounded, who were scattered throughout the huts of Frenchtown. The Indians were gone, but later Darnell learned from the doctor that Procter had promised them a "frolic" that night at Stoney Creek, only six miles away—a short distance for a drunken Indian. Everyone in Frenchtown —townsmen, Americans wounded and whole, and the four Canadians of the guard—spent an uneasy night, listening and hearing in their fear the approach of a red horde.

The Indians came in the morning. They were still a little drunk and very thirsty from their "frolic." Yesterday's enemies, some of them dead from wounds, were still in Frenchtown. To the Indians, each American represented plunder in clothes and pocket, and a scalp for which the British colonel would give money with which to buy more rum, or whisky, or fiery hot French brandy. So the Indians, about two hundred in number, ranged through the town. Major Reynolds was pushed aside, and the interpreters, recognizing the inevitable, removed themselves into the houses. The Indians knifed Captain Hickman on the bed where he lay, ripped off his scalp, and lurched out of the door. At other houses other drunken Indians dragged their victims out of doors to kill them. The native French of Frenchtown either cowered, helpless, or feigned friendship, giving the Indians their brandy and gifts. Captain Nathan Hart was the most prominent of all the wounded from yesterday's battle. His sister had married Senator Henry Clay and he had commanded a company of the elite Lexington Light Infantry in the two battles on the River Raisin. Hart had bribed a friendly Potawatomi to get a horse and help him escape. But they were not yet out of the village before a Wyandot overtook them. The captain was butchered and the Potawatomi and the Wyandot were left to haggle over the victim's possessions and his scalp.

Elias Darnell, with his brother Allen, fared better. He persuaded the Indian who found them that they were both more valuable as prisoners than as scalps. So the brothers, one wounded and one well, stood in the cold at a corner of the house and watched the horror around them. Their captor, guarding his property, sat contently by, turning the wondrous pages of a book of John Wesley's sermons that Elias had had in his pack. When all was done that they wanted to do in the settlement of Frenchtown, the Indians went away. They took the road to Brownstown and on to Malden to sell their scalps and trade their loot and ransom their prisoners. Allen Darnell did not get to Malden. Separated from his brother, the wounded man could not keep up the pace of march, and he was tomahawked as a useless crippled thing. Elias saw the Indian tying Allen's hair to a trophy stick as they walked along. The Indians took Elias to a longhouse outside the walls of Fort Amherst and kept him nearly naked while an old woman grinned and leered at him from a dark corner. In spite of the cold, Elias Darnell escaped in the night to the British, who hid him in the jail and would not give him up.

General Winchester's Second Army of the Northwest was dead on the River Raisin, where, as the fighting left wing of General Harrison's force, it never should have gone. Only the prisoners at Malden remained to be disposed of by Colonel Procter, whose careless contempt for the Yankee wounded had caused the butchery at Frenchtown. For Procter's prisoners one more long horror was waiting: the cold was bitter and the snow deep on the road along the Thames River to the cities of the east. The Americans marched it in their tatters, taunted by their British guards. Captain Dolson, in charge of the prisoners, was detested for his baseness and his cruelty. At a rest halt he jeered at the men, saying that their "General" Harrison soon would be walking the same road to prison. James Allen, sitting in the snow by Elias Darnell, rose up and, looking hard at the mounted British captain, said quietly, "and before that your Irish hide will be so riddled that it won't hold hickory nuts." Still unbeaten, the prisoners from the Northwest army marched into captivity.

XXI

The Thaw of 1813

At the River Raisin, James Winchester lost his uniform, his dignity, and his liberty. General Harrison lost there a thousand good soldiers, not including the fussy brigadier general who, in his increasing years, did not match his pace to the stride of time. The lost soldiers, those dead in battle, those killed at Frenchtown, and the five hundred and thirty-five prisoners of war, were nearly all Kentucky men. The four companies of the 17th Infantry had been recruited in Kentucky. The militiamen were of that state and had volunteered to stay on federal duty after their enlistment was up in February. Although the cry "Remember the River Raisin" was loud through all Kentucky, the lost thousand could not immediately be replaced. It was hard to find unencumbered young men to enlist into the ranks of the 17th and 19th Infantry. The potential recruits, like the militiamen, were needed at home as working sons or hired hands for the spring planting. So General Harrison was obliged to wait until summer to replace the good men lost at the River Raisin before he could carry out his orders to regain Detroit and to invade Upper Canada. Harrison was even hard pressed to hold his early winter gains, the position on the Maumee Rapids that Winchester had weakened in answering the cry for help that came from Frenchtown.

General Harrison was in the saddle with only a small escort behind him when he talked to the first frightened soldier he met fleeing the battle at Frenchtown. On receiving General Winchester's message that he was going to the River Raisin, Harrison was alarmed and he reacted at once. He was at upper Sandusky with the artillery. He ordered all the available guns to go at once to the rapids, sixty miles away. He himself went galloping down the road to lower Sandusky, where General Simon Perkins had a ready regiment of Ohioans of the Western Reserve and a battalion of good Pennsylvanians. Harrison, riding in a sleigh, started for the River Raisin with these troops. Word of Lewis's initial victory reached the commander while on the road along the margin of Lake Erie. The news, instead of reassuring Harrison, increased his concern. Borrowing a horse, he left Perkins and pressed on over the snowy road to the Maumee. Colonel Wells of the 17th was there, and he poured out his own anxiety for the army at Frenchtown, an anxiety that the general shared. On a fresh horse, Harrison pressed on for the River Raisin, to lend his presence to the troops who, like a shot arrow, lay vulnerable and spent, far from the bow that impelled it.

Harrison was not far down the road from the Maumee when he met the first fugitive. There are always those who flee, bearing exaggerated tales of woe. Harrison rode on. Then he met others, pitifully few, who told him of the attack that had routed the right wing, and of the Indians who had gained the south shore of the river. These men knew what they had seen, and Harrison knew, too, what had happened. There was much that now must be done to hold the Maumee Rapids. Harrison turned back. With him were the thirty-three survivors of the thousand men who had fought on the River Raisin.

On the south bank of the Maumee River, below the Rapids and downriver from Hull's old campsite, where, a long time ago, he had fought beside Wayne, Harrison built Fort Meigs. Hacked out of the frozen ground, the earth and log walls encompassed eight acres, behind which were blockhouses, gun platforms, barracks, and warehouses. The men worked hard to secure themselves and their position. The work progressed, blessed by a generally mild winter and by the energy of Captain Eleazar Wood, who, six years earlier, had been graduated from the new military academy at West Point. General Harrison watched the work progressing, received the new guns from the Sandusky park, and planned his offensive. As long as the ice was a bridge from the Michigan shore to Fort Malden, the general kept to his purpose of a winter attack. He also prepared for a summer campaign if that should be necessary.

Frozen hard in the winter ice at Malden lay important elements of the Canadian navy on the upper lakes. The destruction of those vessels before the melting of the ice freed them would mean that the Americans would have naval superiority on Lake Erie in the approaching summer. Old General Hull had recognized the American need for open lines across the water and along the shore. Harrison saw dominance of the lake as a necessity for his invasion of Canada.

Destruction of the Malden flotilla would forward that end by giving the American navy, now building behind Presque Isle, a chancy battle to win the lake.

Harrison planned the raid in detail with Captain Angus Langham of the 19th Infantry and an itinerant French artilleryman whose practical knowledge of incendiary machines was profound. On 2 March, one hundred and seventy men set out, carrying fire bombs, dressed especially in dark clothes for night work and their feet muffled in silent, padded moccasins that gave firm footing on slippery ice. They took rations for six days. Harrison had an anxious wait while the men were gone. He chose to wait on Maumee Bay with a support party to help the raiders back. Captain Langham returned on the second day with all his men. He told Harrison that the ice in the Detroit River was breaking up, that the channel was already open. They had arrived too late to burn the Canadian ships, now safe across the void of black water and grinding floes of ice.

For General Harrison all hopes for a winter campaign were gone. He left the Maumee. He left Fort Meigs. The work of the commanding officer in the west was now with the governments of the states and the nation. The targets of the general's energy must now be the men in assembly who must provide the money to pay for the men and materiel for the next effort to carry the war to the enemy. Too, General Harrison had a family staying in Cincinnati, and he knew they were plagued by illness. The early thaw gave him the opportunity to spend a few days with them as father and husband.

Harrison returned to Cincinnati a major general, the junior

of four commissioned on 2 March in Washington City. The promotion only enhanced his authority in the Northwest. There his strength was in the confidence of the western governors and the eagerness with which the hitherto (and elsewhere) unreliable militiamen followed him, unquestioning, into the face of danger. Less reliant on Harrison's capacity for leadership was John Armstrong, the new Secretary of War. Armstrong sat in the war office, behind a desk too big for his abilities, advised by visitors who were interested only in local and party politics, and revised Harrison's whole army and its policy. The militia, which was already assembling in March 1813, was to be dismissed as unreliable. Hull's two colonels, McArthur and Cass, had told the Secretary how wretched the western militiamen were as soldiers. Instead of the militia, Armstrong decided that six regiments of regulars would constitute the Army of the Northwest, to hold the Ohio posts and the western forts against Indian uprisings, and to regain Michigan and attack Canada. Colonels McArthur and Cass were each to command a brigade in the new regular army of the Northwest. A force of six thousand regulars, well led throughout and whetted keen by training, could do the job. But three of Secretary Armstrong's regiments, the 26th, the 27th, and the 28th, were only numbers on his list, and the 17th and 19th were far below their authorized strength of one thousand each. The 24th Infantry was still recruiting and training in southern Ohio.

John Armstrong also had a new tactical plan. Harrison must move his men and base and all his supplies to Cleveland to the east. From there he was to attack across Lake Erie. The lake crossing would be made safe by the American fleet, as yet unbuilt, which would defeat the existing and increasing British fleet in a future battle.

Presented with Armstrong's unrealistic plans in the form of orders from Washington, General Harrison defied them. Backed by the western governors, of whom he was one, and supported by the strong western congressmen, General Harrison continued to employ the militiamen he had raised and to use regulars who walked on the solid ground of fact. In mid-March General Harrison wrote with restraint to the Secretary of War. He then carried on with his plans, based on the Maumee Rapids. The American fleet was still a tantalizing hope, unfounded in fact.

All through March Harrison's leave with his family consisted of days snatched at random, interrupted by the arrival and departure of messengers. On 2 April the Pennsylvania and Virginia militia at Fort Meigs would be going home as time-expired men. Harrison had started the 19th Infantry toward that fort. He himself must be there at the end of the month with reinforcements plucked from all the small posts on the supply lines throughout Ohio. The governor of Kentucky had promised fifteen hundred militiamen under Brigadier General Green Clay in April. They, the Kentuckians, and all the men Harrison could find would be needed at Fort Meigs before the ice was gone from the Detroit River and the English and the Indians came. There were indications that spring was coming early in 1813.

Tecumseh was ready for the hurrying spring. He had been lying ill in a distant village, to which he had gone recruiting, when the battle of the River Raisin was fought. Had he been at Frenchtown he might have averted the killing of the wounded there. But his winter trip to the Indian villages near and far had produced a promised band of almost twenty-four hundred warriors. Those who arrived early in April prowled the woods around Fort Meigs. They killed two wanderers from the fort and took two prisoners before General Harrison arrived on 12 April and the turnover of troops was completed. The fort was secure and strong, and able to hold out until the promised Kentuckians arrived.

Procter, too, was ready for the melting of the ice to give up the imprisoned fleet and the boats to take his soldiers to the mouth of the Maumee for an attack on Fort Meigs. Brigadier General Procter (he had been promoted) boarded *Lady Prevost* on 24 April. He had aboard and on the other vessels some five hundred regulars and nearly as many militia. The Indians, under Tecumseh and Round Head, were going overland to terrify by their passing the citizens of Michigan who were under British martial law. Procter moved slowly to the Maumee, making a detour on the way to visit the great camp of the Indians, where he promised that his guns would soon smoke the long knives from their hive and that there would be much honey to share.

On 28 April an Ohio captain, scouting downriver, discovered the British and Canadian troops landing near the ruins of Fort Miami. Later in the day an alert gunner at Fort Meigs saw a small party of mounted men observing the fort. Through a spyglass it was easy to make out the Indian as Tecumseh. He was handsomely dressed and ornamented and sat straight and haughty, on a fine horse. By the youthfulness of his bearing and the deference the others gave him, Procter was easily identified beside the great Shawnee leader. A cannon shot from the fort fell close enough to the horsemen to send the group away at a fast canter. In the meantime, Captain Mathew Dixon of the Royal Engineers was across the Maumee, driving stakes to mark a battery to "smoke out" the defenders of the fort.

General Harrison, walking the confines of the walls, was ready to be besieged. Captain Wood had built a good fort, well ditched without, strong palisaded walls, well-sited gun platforms, ample space and buildings within. The great mass of Indians whom he knew to be with Tecumseh encouraged Harrison. All the Indian fighting men unfriendly to the Americans were in front of him. None were left to harass his rear, to attack the western forts, to maraud the farther settlements. Before the siege closed in, Harrison sent a message ordering up troops that had been assigned a defensive role. To the eleven hundred Americans waiting in Fort Meigs to receive the enemy, General Harrison addressed a most eloquent general order. The gunners, piling shot beside their run-out guns, heard the order read to them. Work parties, pausing to lean on their shovels, listened to their officers repeat the general's stirring words. All, as they could, looked across the Maumee to the battlefield of Fallen Timbers. In his general order Harrison had invoked that ground and had given them as their own the heritage of Wayne's victory. All the soldiers at Fort Meigs knew that their general had been at Fallen Timbers, and the tradition born to American arms that day was his to give and theirs to enhance. All knew that Brigadier General Clay was coming from the west to join them with fifteen hundred men. The gate guard had allowed the messengers summoning Clay to hurry out and then had barred the gate behind them.

XXII

Out of the Forest, Onto the Lake

The couriers found Brigadier General Green Clay at Fort Winchester. He was dressed in his hunting shirt, ready for the river. His two regiments were loading the eighteen scows that would carry them downstream. The boats were soon away, though night was falling before they reached the head of the rapids eighteen miles above Fort Meigs. The river, high with the last of the spring runoff, moved swiftly through rocks and shallows beyond where General Clay, his colonels, the pilots of the boats, and the couriers stood on the riverbank. In the far distance the faint sound of gunfire marked the place of siege. Dark clouds were gathering, following the setting of a young moon. The river pilots were adamant: they could not take the big scows down the rapids on such a dark night. Resigned, General Clay gave the order to bivouac and turned to the couriers, leaning on their long rifles and listening to the thump of the guns far away. Yes, they would return to Fort Meigs that night with Clay's message of encouragement to Harrison and the besieged garrison. The two brave men slipped away.

The bivouac quieted down. General Clay rolled up in his three blankets. There was no light for the general to read from his copy of *MacKensie's Travels*. He slept until the rain began to fall.

The relief force passed the rapids in the rain of the early dawn of 5 May. Colonel William Dudley flew his regiment's flag on the lead boat. It was the first thing the two officers from Fort Meigs saw as they paddled the light canoe up the Maumee. Swinging in close alongside, the officers told the colonel that the couriers had gotten through and that they carried orders from Harrison for General Clay. To the greetings of Dudley's men, the two passed up the line to the thirteenth scow, where Clay was riding. They told the general that Fort Meigs held firm. A traverse had been built to minimize the effect of gunfire from the north shore and from the new battery east of the fort on the right bank. There had been few casualties and little real damage in the fort, considering the number of shells thrown by the British in the five days since the bombardment had begun. It was the general's intent to sortie that day against the enemy's east battery. Harrison requested General Clay to detach eight hundred men to attack and spike the guns of the British battery on the north shore and, once successful, to cross the Maumee immediately to the safety of Fort Meigs. The rest of Clay's force was to land on the right bank above the fort, fight through the screen of Tecumseh's Indians, and join up with another sortie coming to help them in. The main body of the British and Canadians was still downriver at the ruins of Fort Miami.

Clay gave the big north battery to Colonel Dudley's

regiment. Eagerly and quickly, the Kentuckians and their bold colonel found a landing place and ran their boats onto it. They were gone, vanished into the woods, before the sixth scow and the last of Clay's other, smaller, regiment passed by. Dudley's plan was to divide his troops into a stop force between the battery and Fort Miami, while he, with the main body, attacked the guns from the west. Captain Leslie Combs, with thirty rangers and seven friendly Indians, well identified, would patrol behind the battery to divert any British Indians annoying the Americans' flank.

All went well as Dudley led his men, howling and yelling, into the battery. Stunned, the British gunners surrendered. From the grand battery Harrison saw the Union Jack hauled down, and he began the preparation to get the men back over the Maumee. Dudley, his men wandering around the gun pits admiring the big 24-pounders, long twelves, and squat and chunky howitzers and mortars, had a problem. No one had brought along the gun spikes of the special design and metal that, once driven into the touchholes, would keep the pieces out of action for days. The American officers were contriving spikes from ramrods when firing broke out in the woods. Combs's men had found Indians and were having sport with them. Some of Dudley's men drifted off to join Combs. The orders were to spike the guns and retire. But Combs had misinterpreted the last part of his instructions. He did not retire. Word came to Dudley that Combs was hard pressed. With the impetuosity that marked the Kentucky militiaman of 1812 and 1813, and his only fault as a soldier, Dudley led his men to the rescue. The rescue was unnecessary. With the arrival of reinforcements Combs's holding action developed into an attack, the attack into a rout of the Indians, and the rout into a wild pursuit, to the cry, "Remember the River Raisin." The Kentuckians, three-quarters of Dudley's force, were well on the way toward Fort Miami, scattered widely through the brush and woods. So three companies of the 41st Foot, under the tight control of Major Muir, found the Americans. They attacked, and with the Indians, now encouraged, hunted down the disorganized regiment of Kentucky men. Dudley was last seen, a fleshy, desperate man, already twice wounded, twisting on the ground, fighting a losing battle against a yowling group of Indians. Captain Combs, though wounded, was luckier. He surrendered to the white men. But his safety was brief. He and the other prisoners were given under the guard of Indians. Procter, since Frenchtown a brigadier general, gave his prisoners only a token guard of white soldiers. Within a double line of Indians the disarmed rabble of nearly six hundred Americans were prodded and poked and snatched at as they were driven back to Fort Miami.

At the fort they were herded into the ruins. Their Indian guards crowded in to scavenge clothes and shoes and trinkets from their pockets. When some of the Indians under Tecumseh were moved over from the south shore they, too, entered the fort. They had missed the battle and were angry and greedy. The fighting began, armed Indians against barehanded Kentuckians. A British soldier of the 41st, an older man named Russell, dashed in to the developing melee, his rifle butt swinging in aid of the defenseless prisoners. An Indian shot him through the heart. From his camp near by, General Procter let the Indian allies have their way, a way which he hesitated to stop. Not Tecumseh, who had just come from

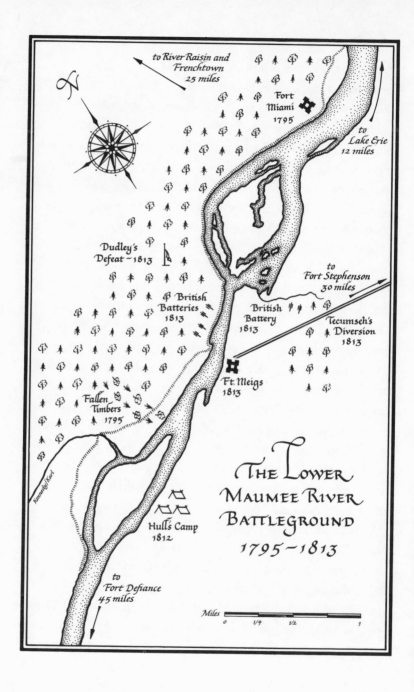

to River Raisin and
Frenchtown
25 miles

Fort
Miami
1795

to
Lake Erie
12 miles

Dudley's
Defeat – 1813

British
Batteries
1813

British
Battery
1813

to
Fort Stephenson
30 miles

Tecumseh's
Diversion
1813

Ft. Meigs
1813

Fallen
Timbers
1795

Kennedy Hart

Hull's Camp
1812

The Lower
Maumee River
Battleground
1795–1813

to
Fort Defiance
45 miles

Miles
0   1/4   1/2   1

across the river. He kicked his horse into a gallop, and with his own tomahawk slashing, he charged, shouting "Cease" into the frenzied mob. Gradually he quieted them, and with Colonel Elliott, he drove the Indians out of the fort. While the Americans were still sorting their dead from their wounded, Tecumseh rode off, still at a gallop, to find and confront Procter for a coward and a craven to have done nothing. Having vented his contempt and anger, Tecumseh stalked off in disdain.

General Harrison stood on the rain-soaked grand battery. General Clay had arrived, and he stood beside his commander, holding his umbrella. They watched as the signal calling Colonel Dudley back was repeated and ignored. Distant rifle and musket fire marked the course of Dudley's attack, pursuit, and disobedience. Soon firing broke out around the battery where the Kentuckian had left a quarter of his force to guard the spiked guns. Captain Dixon, the engineer, well-reinforced, was counterattacking to regain his battery. The watchers on the bastion saw the guard fleeing toward the river and the Union Jack run up again over the British battery. By night the first of the ineptly spiked guns was again in action.

The refugees of the battery guard, perhaps two hundred men, mostly wounded, were in the fort when Harrison stalked through to another quarter of the wall. He counted as lost Dudley and six hundred men. There was one other operation planned for this day, 5 May. Harrison turned his full attention to it. Near the mortar bastion at the southeast corner of Fort Meigs, Colonel John Miller of the 19th Infantry waited with three hundred and fifty Stormers to go against the 3-gun battery south and east of the fort. Captain Langham, who had tried to burn the British boats, was with the colonel. Young

Captain Wilson Elliott was going with the Stormers, commanding volunteers from his own company of the 19th. Somewhere out there he might meet his uncle, Colonel Matthew Elliott, the Indian Agent of ill fame. An American artillery officer was with Miller's party. He carried spikes and a hammer to drive them well home. General Harrison arrived, spoke briefly, and the Stormers were off, out of the gate, and, forming quickly, running across the cleared ground. Near the battery they halted, fired a volley, and behind Colonel Miller went in, around, and over the walls behind their bayonets. Quickly the gun, the mortar, and the howitzer were spiked. Their job done, Colonel Miller called his men together and ordered the withdrawal. They came back, walking across the cleared level ground, with its strange, enemy view of the outside of the walls of their fort. With them as they passed in through the gate to the familiar interior were forty-one awed British prisoners of war, among them two subalterns.

The rainy day of 5 May ended, and with it ended the siege. For three more days of desultory exchange of cannonfire passed between the fort and the batteries. For three days, flags of truce and parley passed between Procter and Harrison. Surrender demands were made and refused. The exchange of prisoners was arranged with care. The Americans within Fort Meigs had withstood the worst the British could do. They could and would hold on. The Indians had had their day of battle. They had their scalps, their loot, their prisoners, and enough of campaigning with the British. They wandered off to their homes. Tecumseh was left alone with less than a hundred of his chiefs and warriors, still dedicated, as was he, to the dream of a united Indian empire. Procter, too, was feeling the futility of the three dragging days following the sorties and battles. The sixteen hundred shells he had hurled into Fort Meigs had not smoked the enemy from their hive. The officers of Canadian militia were coming to his tent with tales of the failure of the early crop. Their men must soon go home for the planting or else the west of Upper Canada would starve when winter came. From the east came word that Fort George on the Niagara River had fallen to the Yankees, and that all roads west to Amherstburg and Detroit were threatened. On 9 May the British commander and all his remaining men sailed back to Fort Malden. There Procter was behind the shield of the Lake Erie fleet. The new brig *Detroit,* of which much was expected, was still on the ways at Fort Malden.

Two days after Procter sailed out of the mouth of the Maumee River, Harrison left Fort Meigs. General Clay and all the defenders remained at the staunch fort which was the pivot of the general's whole northern line of defense and attack. Harrison rode eastward across the Black Swamp toward the Sandusky River. That was the place on the long Lake Erie shore frontier where he expected Procter's next strike from across the lake. General Harrison's plans for an overland, over-ice campaign had failed to develop. With spring and open water he was forced into a waiting defensive. He must wait while his new army of regular soldiers was raised and trained, before he could take the offensive against Canada and liberate occupied Michigan. Now that the twenty-three-year war for the American Northwest had moved out of the forest and off the rivers onto the littoral of Lake Erie, Harrison must have a navy. The British had a fleet that roamed at will over the lake. In the spring of 1813 General Harrison, like Hull before him, still waited for the American fleet to be built. That fleet must win a decisive battle over the British fleet before Harrison's army could move with safety to an attack of Canada either across the wide lake or around the shore.

The American fleet promised for June was many weeks from completion when May ended. Although General Harrison's offensive plans and orders depended on the fleet, the protection of the shipyard, since it was in Pennsylvania, was out of the area of his responsibility. Presque Isle and its naval preparations were guarded by Pennsylvania militiamen against the ever imminent attack from the lake. However, in General Harrison's military district, now designated the Eighth, there were the three possible bases from which an amphibious attack could be launched against the western Canadian shore. Far to the east was the shore city of Cleveland, which the Secretary of War favored and which Harrison opposed because it was more than a hundred miles from his firm base at Fort Meigs. Seventy miles west of Cleveland was Sandusky Bay, a likely place to begin naval operations and the loading of the transports. It was a protected harbor at the head of the Sandusky River, an established supply line and close enough to Fort Meigs for support. Harrison himself favored the mouth of the Maumee for the launching point of his attack by water and also for the cavalry which would have to go by land to a ferry point on the west bank of the Detroit River.

Through the warm days of May and June, General Harrison concentrated his attention on defending the threatened lake shore and on organizing his invasion force of regulars. Elsewhere in his Eighth Military District things were quiet and orderly. The Indians who were hostile were all in front of the Maumee line of forts, rallying once again to Tecumseh. From Fort Wayne Colonel Richard Johnson, a member of Congress, and eight hundred mounted Kentuckians on federal service kept the peace eastward from the upper Wabash to the lake. Beyond the Wabash, Brigadier General Benjamin Howard was Harrison's deputy commander in the far west territory, over which Howard was also governor. Brevet Major Zachary Taylor, the defender of Fort Harrison, was with Howard, carrying on counter raids against British-inspired Indians, just as in the old times along the Ohio frontier. East of the Wabash and north of the Ohio River, the territory was secure against marauding war parties as far north as the Michigan border and the southern shore of Lake Erie. Treaties between the United States and the Indian nations living there formed a basis for peace between the white man and the red. Stockaded forts and blockhouses threaded the treaty lands, assuring the peace. Although the councils of the nations were friendly, Tecumseh and his exiled warriors still dreamed of an Indian homeland in the American Northwest. General Harrison respected his Indian rival for the Northwest. He kept his blockhouses well manned. Across the lake, he faced his last and oldest enemy, the British.

Militiamen serving "Uncle Sam" sat out their months of enlistment in the boredom of the blockhouse and the confines of the clearing around the palisade. By their presence they kept open the supply routes to the regulars and the militiamen on federal service who were holding on the line. Recruits for the regulars came out of the forest, crossed the clearing past the loiterers at the open gate, disappeared into the forest, and were gone. A wagon train would stop and, outside the palisade, give their lean cattle a day of grazing. The militiamen sought out the drovers for a scrap of gossip from the world from which they had come. Best of all were the express riders who stopped for a change of mounts and a hasty meal. They brought news of the army, the enemy, the Indians, and General Harrison.

Toward the end of June the numbers of messengers suddenly increased, and the flood of rumors quickened. Tecumseh's Indians were gathering in their thousands along the Detroit River. The British fleet was back from a cruise to the east. General Harrison was at Fort Meigs, which was threatened. Colonel Johnson and all his horsemen had met Harrison at Fort Meigs. They had conferred with General Clay. Harrison had gone to Cleveland to inspect and alert the defenses there. The militiamen in the scattered forts looked to their own safety and argued over where Procter and Tecumseh would strike their expected blow. Fort Meigs? Sandusky Bay? Cleveland? Or even Erie, far to the east and out of their care?

General Harrison still believed that the next attack would fall on lower Sandusky, where little Fort Stephenson stood at the head of navigation up the Sandusky River. In July he moved his headquarters to the Seneca Towns, ten easy miles south of Fort Stephenson, and ordered the concentration of his force. Colonel William Anderson came to the Seneca Towns, with his new 24th Regiment of U.S. Infantry, still raw, still ragged, but making into regulars. Colonel Wells brought his veterans of the 17th. McArthur and Cass were coming. Major Ball and a hundred and fifty men of his 2nd Regiment of Light Dragoons came. They were sent on east to Cleveland, in case

Harrison was wrong. Colonel Johnson and his regiment of mounted Kentuckians were coming to take up a position between Fort Stephenson and Cleveland, as a mobile reserve for both places. First, however, Johnson was to lead his men from Fort Winchester, where he was, in a wide arc through Michigan to the Raisin River, to assess the strength and imminence of the Indian-British-Canadian attack. His report bought time for Harrison, as Tecumseh and Procter were not yet ready to lash out. They would not come until late in July, and by then the call-out of the Ohio militia would be complete. Johnson and his long column of horsemen, who had ridden hard and had been many long days in the saddle, set out for their station on the Huron River, east of lower Sandusky.

The Kentuckians, riding at an easy walk, arrived at Fort Stephenson on Independence Day. The fort was dressed for a gala. Flags flew from the three blockhouses and from the angles of the palisade. The one old 6-pounder was charged for a salute in honor of the day. A scratch band made music by the fort's main gate. George Croghan was the commander of the fort, a veteran of Tippecanoe, where he had been aide to Harrison, and now, at twenty-one, a major of the 17th Infantry. Croghan had prepared an address to stir the high ardor of his garrison of one hundred and sixty regulars to an even higher pitch. But when Johnson, distinguished colonel and eminent member of the Congress, arrived, the young major deferred to him. It was Congressman Johnson who exhorted the men of the two commands, praising the day and dedicating the deeds of the past to "doers of the deeds yet to be done" for the glory of the nation. That evening Major

Croghan was host at a dinner. He called many toasts from the officers invited, while the men of the two commands fraternized in the barracks and at the bivouac fires. Nearly eight hundred horses cropped contentedly on the new grass in the darkness outside Fort Stephenson.

XXIII

Attack by Ruse and by Storm

Two months after his proclaimed victory over Dudley on 5 May, General Procter had more Indians around Amherstburg than he had had at the siege of Fort Meigs. Tecumseh's warriors in exile had returned, ready again to make war. The venerable Round Head was still in the Michigan towns across the Detroit River, his young men of the northern nations restless for more war. New Indians, fierce men, still untainted by close proximity to the white man's culture, had come to Fort Malden to do war along with their British brothers. Robert Dickson, the newly appointed agent to the farther nations, had persuaded them to come east from their homelands in the forests west of Lake Michigan and the Mississippi at the edge of the Great Plains. Already they had clashed with Governor Howard's westering Americans, and they had heeded Dickson's call to better fighting, more loot, greater glory with Tecumseh and the British. A thousand warriors met at the rendezvous he had set at burned-out Fort Dearborn on the Chicago River. Dickson was there to lead them across the base of the Michigan Peninsula. On their way the western Indians missed Colonel Johnson and his patrolling horsemen.

With a force of upward of four thousand Indians centered around Fort Malden, General Procter was faced with the decision of how, when, where to use them. Soon their patience, always short, would wear thin, and they would go home, or go raiding where they willed, which might be anywhere. Restless bands of Indians were already prowling around Fort Meigs. The happiest of them returned with six raw scalps from a fatigue party surprised near the fort. General Procter, always uncertain and particularly cowed by his Indian allies delayed and vacillated and came to no decision.

The plan and the scheme to attack Fort Meigs was Tecumseh's, and he overawed the young British general into accepting and co-operating with it. The Shawnee's plan was a ruse to lure the Americans from Fort Meigs for the humanitarian reasons that Tecumseh recognized as his enemy's greatest weakness in war. On the day chosen, his Indians would stage a sham battle on the road to Sandusky, out of sight but well within hearing from the fort. The defenders of Fort Meigs, according to the pattern of Yankee behavior, would pour out of the fort to the aid and rescue of their supposed friends. General Procter's regulars and Canadians, hidden in the gully behind the old mortar battery, would attack the relief force on the flank. The Indians staging the sham battle would abandon their theatrics and fall upon the Americans. Other Indians around Fort Meigs would attack and, they hoped, would rush through the opened gate. There were two thousand men in the fort and five months' provisions. There would be booty enough for all.

On the afternoon of 26 July all was in readiness, and at sunset Tecumseh began the sham fight on the Sandusky road. General Clay and his officers hurried to the southern bastion. Drums in the fort beat the assembly. The soldiers hurried to their rally points, ready to sortie. On the bastion Clay listened calmly to the swelling sounds of musketfire in the distance. Battalion commanders climbed the ramp to where the general stood, reported their commands assembled, and asked for orders to go out. The war whoops and shouts of the Indians took on a note of victory as they seemingly closed in on the Americans fighting to get to the fort. The officers around Clay demanded that they be permitted to go to the rescue before it was too late. General Clay stood firm on his refusal to let his soldiers sortie. Harrison had been in close touch with Fort Meigs and had told Clay that no force would be sent, that his post was to be defended closely, and to beware of surprise. With darkness and a shower of rain, Tecumseh called off the sham fight. General Clay stood the assembly down and went to an uneasy dinner. He could not yet know that he had been right.

Five days later an American reconnaissance party on the shore of Sandusky Bay saw a British flotilla of odd craft, shepherded by gunboats, enter the Bay. There was no sighting of the big vessels of the British fleet. Procter, after being bullied into trying Tecumseh's scheme, had come at last to the Sandusky River. The British general reckoned that Fort Stephenson, the small fort at the head of navigation, would fall to an assault by his regulars. Although the heavier guns of the fleet would have helped shoot the storming party in, the big vessels were away to the east, and for his bombardment Procter would have to rely on the five mobile 6-pounders mounted on the gunboats.

The British landed on 1 August. Painted Indians met them on the shore and led the orderly companies of redcoated soldiers around through a small wood to the gully from which their assault would start. From all around the fort the marching men of the 41st Foot could hear the musketfire of their Indian allies. For several days the warriors of the nations had been at the fort, annoying the defenders. The chiefs at the landing place told Procter that the soldiers within the fort were prisoners, waiting to be slaughtered. Procter watched as gunners brought the howitzer ashore. The chiefs told him that General Harrison was ten miles away, cowering in a fortified camp. One of the field guns opened the cannonading of the fort from a gunboat in the river. The shot whooshed high over General Procter's head. He turned to watch it strike.

Even before the first of Tecumseh's Indians came to the Sandusky, General William Henry Harrison had given up Fort Stephenson as not worth holding. He was having trouble getting his troop to the assembly, and George Croghan's hundred and sixty men of the 17th Infantry could be better deployed in the armed camp at the Seneca Towns. Colonel George Paull's Recruit Regiment, the 27th, had arrived and Colonel Theodore Dey Owing's 28th Infantry, soon expected, would probably be as raw and untrained as Paull's. The hardest blow to Harrison's defense of the Lake Erie shore came from Washington City, where the sharp end of a quill pen killed at distances unimagined by a Kentucky rifleman. Secretary of War Armstrong, by a direct order, had sent

Johnson and his eight hundred mounted riflemen to Illinois. The Secretary, in the wisdom and the power of his office, knew that Indian Agent Dickson had raised the savage western nations against General and Governor Howard's troops and citizens there. Although Johnson protested the order to his friend Harrison, and Harrison knew that Dickson's Indians were then on the Detroit River, the orders were not to be tampered with, not even by a popular general in the field. Twice General Harrison had intentionally misinterpreted Secretary Armstrong's orders, once by bringing Clay's militiamen to Fort Meigs, and a second time by retaining Ohio militiamen for the defense of the Erie shore. Harrison could not be disobedient again. So Johnson reluctantly started off on the long ride to western Illinois.

General Harrison himself was faced with an incident of disobedience in his own command. When he had decided to give up Fort Stephenson, he sent young Croghan specific orders to burn and blow up the place at the first appearance of Procter. Unfortunately, Harrison had added a discretionary clause about the "vanity" of attempting a retreat in the face of an Indian force. That rider was enough excuse for Croghan. When a peremptory order came to "abandon the fort at once," Major Croghan calmly replied that the order had come too late and that "we have determined to maintain this place, and, by heaven! we can." Harrison, the general, was furious. But he recognized in Major Croghan the boy of his own youth and a nephew worthy of Croghan's uncle, George Rogers Clark.

In the months of his command of Fort Stephenson, Major Croghan had had his hundred and sixty men dig a wide and deep ditch outside the picket walls. He also built a third blockhouse to enfilade the ditch under the south and west walls. Into the reinforced second story of the blockhouse in the center of the north face, Major Croghan moved his one old iron 6-pounder. The gun covered the whole north ditch. Into the second story of this gun tower he gathered his ammunition and a miscellany of old metal scraps in lieu of the grape and canister shot that was not in his arsenal.

The arrival of the Indians discommoded Croghan not at all. They kept their distance and their musketfire had no effect either on the log walls or on the well-trained soldiers, to whom unnecessary risk was foolhardy. Like Procter, Major Croghan watched with interest the first fall of the shot from the gunboats down the river. The walls of the fort were made of thick logs, sunk vertically into the ground, and the 6-pound shot struck them, but it merely bounced off and fell back into the ditch. The howitzer, too, had no effect on Fort Stephenson. During the night of 1 August Croghan and his men, keeping an alert watch, could hear what they guessed was the British moving the field guns from the boats to the edge of the wood to the north.

On the morning of 2 August three guns were in place and the parley drums were beat from Procter's lines. Out of the gully to the north of Fort Stephenson, parading behind the beating drums, marched old Colonel Elliott, the Indian Agent; Major Dixon, the redcoated Royal engineer officer; and Captain Peter Chambers of the Thames River valley, representing the Canadian militia. Against this British array of rank, age, and prominence, Major Croghan sent his most junior subaltern, Second Lieutenant Edmund Shipp, Jr., of Kentucky. The object of the parley was to demand surrender of the fort and garrison. It was Shipp's duty to refuse. The very old Elliott sought to intimidate the saucy young subaltern. Chambers adopted a paternal role. Dixon played the cultured English gentleman, who pleaded with the boy in the name of humanity not to let the savages perpetrate yet another slaughter. Lieutenant Shipp, standing straight and slim and alone, assured the gentlemen that there would be no massacre. Should the British and their Indians ever get into the fort, no defender would be alive to kill. The parley ended with polite bows all around.

When the parley drums were silent and the truce flags down, Procter began his cannonade. For most of the day shot, from less than a three-hundred-yard range, pounded the pickets of Fort Stephenson. Inside, the Americans waited patiently under cover and did not deign to reply to the British with gun or musket. Enough riflemen stood on guard at the loopholes to keep the Indians back, away from the ditch. From the northeast bastion a crouching sentry watched an Indian slowly climb a tall tree that grew on the river plain below the fort. Quietly, the sentry watched as the man climbed higher and higher up the ladder of branches. When the Indian was higher than the wall and could look inside, the soldier carefully figured windage and distance, aimed slowly, held on, and fired. When the smoke drifted by he automatically reloaded his slim brown rifle as he watched the Indian tumble slowly down, down through the branches that clutched at the red body in its slow plunge to the ground below. Major Croghan walked the rounds inside the wall, standing for a moment or two with a sentry at his loophole, visiting the wounded, counting now upward to a final count of seven, and arranging for the care of

the one soldier who had been killed. In his rounds of the
picket, Croghan carefully tested the set of the logs in the
ground at the northwest corner. Where the shells struck
hardest several were loose in their footings. Some were leaning
inward at the top. Croghan called up a work party and from
the storehouse he issued bags of flour. While the 6-pound
shells thumped against the outside, with the sacks he braced the
wall from the inside. The wall would hold. Croghan climbed
up into the north blockhouse, where a gun crew of Pittsburgh
volunteers had been waiting all the long day beside their iron
6-pounder.

The hour had gone past four. Stormheads were gathering in
the west. The low rumbling of thunder underscored the
intermittent beat of the British cannon. A restless rustling
wind was blowing the gunsmoke toward the fort. Behind the
billowing screen General Procter was hurrying the preparations of the storming party. Procter must take Fort Stephenson
before General Harrison could reinforce and relieve the
garrison. The Grenadiers were gone on the wide march
around the fort to create a diversion in front of the southern
wall. The main attack was ready to go in against the northwest
corner, which Procter had observed was weakened by the
day's bombardment. In the gully, a scant two hundred yards
removed from the northwest corner of the fort, the Stormers
were formed up and ready. Lieutenant Colonel William Short,
with brevet rank, was the officer in command. He led one of
the two columns. A Lieutenant Gordon, also of the 41st Foot,
led the second. Major Muir, Captain Dixon, and other officers
were going along as volunteers. Procter watched from a
vantage point well out of danger. At five o'clock the Pioneers,

carrying their axes, rose up out of the gully and, as is the way of British infantrymen, moved silently and unhurriedly into the smoke. The columns of Stormers, with honed bayonets, came on close behind. The British guns fell silent. Within thirty yards of the ditch the wall of Fort Stephenson took shape through the smoke. The Pioneers tightened their grip on their axes and quickened their pace toward the big logs which they must hew and batter down for the men following close behind.

Major Croghan was waiting and watching. At every loophole along the threatened stretch of wall soldiers waited their turn to fire, give way, reload, and take their turn to fire again. The American small-arms fire began as the first dark loping figure appeared out of the rolling smoke across the ditch. The momentum of the British attack carried the Pioneers into the ditch. Without pause they began their scramble up the inner wall to get their axes to the stakes of the wall. Only feet away, Americans were angling their muskets to fire into the upturned faces of the Britons and Canadians below. Behind the Pioneers, the Stormers were jumping down into the ditch. A few figures lay like dumped gunnysacks on the flat ground beyond.

In the north blockhouse of Fort Stephenson, on the second story, Croghan's single gun had been wheeled around to aim out of the west gunport. The small 6-inch tube, crammed to its mouth with musket balls and scrap iron, was angled steeply down. The Gun Captain, Private Brown, looked quickly through the port into a ditch filled with men in red coats, purposefully going about their business of aiding the Pioneers or firing up to try and clear the loopholes. Private Brown stepped back and, screaming to be heard over the din, gave his order to fire. With a roar and a great puff of smoke, the slugs and ball from the cannon's mouth tore into the mass of men in the deep trench below. On its recoil, the old iron cannon had leaped back into the room. In the powder smoke curling through the room the six Pittsburghers of the crew hurried to reload. Again they filled their piece with scrap metal from a bucket. The cannon was rolled out for a second shot. Lieutenant Gordon's column was now in the ditch, which was a confused mass of jostling men, uninjured, wounded, and dead, the living still striving to get up and tear down the solid wall of logs. The second shot ripped into the British massed in the ditch. They had had enough. The wall stood firm. Any further attempt was useless. Colonel Short was down, sorely wounded. Lieutenant Gordon was dead. Major Muir and Captain Dixon, both wounded, rallied the remnant of the two columns and sent the men scrambling out of the ditch and running back to the safety of the gully. From the desolation in the ditch a sword rose high, on it waved a white handkerchief. Colonel Short was making his plea for mercy for the wounded men and for the whole men who had taken refuge in safe protected angles under the gun embrasure. Behind the wall, Major Croghan ordered the cease fire. He ran over to the south wall, where Captain James Hunter of the 17th had sighted the Grenadier companies deploying. They had come too late for their purpose. A volley from the south wall sent the Grenadiers marching back the way they came.

In the northwest ditch of Fort Stephenson, the British wounded were trapped. Their friends could not come for them; their enemy could not come for them, nor would the enemy let them escape. Indians lay in the bushes throughout the cleared land, keeping the Americans alert behind their wall. Carefully, the Americans let buckets of water down by ropes into the ditch to ease the pain of the Britishers lying there. They called out softly that at nightfall they would come out to rescue them. The storm that had threatened passed by along the lake shore, and the sun finally set through tinted clouds on the Sunday of 2 August. When darkness came, the men of the 17th U.S. Infantry brought the wounded and the prisoners in through a wicket gate. They brought the dead in, too, lest the Indians get to the bodies during the night.

In the night General Procter stole away to his boats and departed the Sandusky River. The Indians, too, were gone in the morning. Major Croghan, satisfied that all the enemy had gone, sat down and wrote a brief note to General Harrison, proclaiming victory. Then, after thirty-six anxious hours, the twenty-one-year-old officer, a new hero to his nation, went to his bed and slept. His official report could wait. The encomiums, the sword of honor, the gold medal presented by Congress, all could wait upon his tiredness.

General Harrison was pleased with his former aide, who had balanced disobedience against the possibility of success and in his self-confidence had won. The Indians were gone and so were the British and Canadians. Watchers on the coast saw them go, sailing and paddling between the point of land that, thumblike, forms Sandusky Bay, and the three Bass Islands out in the lake.

XXIV

Lieutenants, Captains, and Commodores

The United States navy had, in 1812, more captains than it had quarterdecks to put them on, and a greater supply of qualified junior officers than all the captains could ever use. At the beginning of the war with Britain, Oliver Hazard Perry was one of the least notable of the Navy Department's lieutenants. At the age of fourteen, Perry had gone to sea from his home in Newport, Rhode Island, in 1799. He served three years as a midshipman on his father's frigate. At seventeen, Oliver Perry shipped out for the Mediterranean, where he served on frigates, and for a time on the small schooner *Nautilus,* where a midshipman could better gain the notice of his captain. The Mediterranean squadron was a severe testing ground for the world's newest sea power. On the timeless inland sea, where man first launched a boat, Oliver Hazard Perry learned truculence and pride of service to match a seamanship as solid and sure as the rocks of Rhode Island. He did not gain distinction abroad, and his promotion and first command, a 14-gun schooner, did not come until 1809. Two years later, Lieutenant Perry was rotated to command a squadron of gunboats confined to Narragansett Bay. The "gunboat navy" represented President Jefferson's dream of a non-belligerent force, a theory which all but stifled American sea power in its infancy and almost beached forever many men of naval talent. But Lieutenant Perry was one seaman who would not be denied a deck, a sail, and a battery of guns. With little hope of a berth on a frigate at sea, Perry asked for and received employment with the fleet on the inland lakes. Commodore Chauncey accepted the tall, twenty-seven-year-old lieutenant for a particular service: the command of an unbuilt fleet on Lake Erie and on all the upper lakes.

Oliver Hazard Perry brought with him as a present to his commodore one hundred and fifty seamen and three fine sailing masters from his gunboat squadron. For himself, he took along his thirteen-year-old brother, Alexander. After a fortnight with his commodore on Lake Ontario, Captain Perry traveled west with his brother through thawing snow to Buffalo and the first glimpse of the freshwater sea that was his trust. He inspected and left orders at the naval installation at Black Rock, then hastened on. The promise and discouragement of early spring was in the late March air when he arrived at Presque Isle. With Oliver Hazard Perry's arrival hope came to the fleet growing so slowly in the Bay.

Daniel Dobbins, a lake sailor, had chosen for his shipyard the deep water behind a sandbar in the shelter of the headland which was almost an island, and so had been named Presque Isle. Dobbins had been a paroled prisoner from Fort Mackinac. On his release he had gone to Washington to plead for a Lake Erie navy. He had made his point, and had been given the rank of sailing master with funds to build two gunboats. The gunboats would be built at Presque Isle, where the sandbar kept them safe from the big vessels of the Canadian Marine. Work on the two 50-foot keels, begun in October, moved slowly through the approaching winter. Commodore Chauncey, on a December tour of the dockyard, gave Dobbins orders to cut and prepare timbers for two large brigs. In early March, Noah Brown, a New York shipbuilder of accomplishment, arrived at the Pennsylvania town to put the stack of timbers together to form the two brigs. When Perry came to Presque Isle not a vessel was afloat. Dobbins's two gunboats were being planked, Brown had laid the keels of the two 22-gun brigs and a schooner, and ways for a third gunboat were being laid down.

Perry's work was not in the shipyard. That was for the shipwrights and the carpenters, just as the defense of the place was for the Pennsylvania militiamen. Perry's concern was for the men and materiel to sail and to fight his ships. He went to Pittsburgh over the old French portage route from Presque Isle, and there he stayed until mid-April, begging, scrounging, stealing sails and cordage, ironmongery and paint, and all the things ships and men need before putting out in a new craft to do battle. Meanwhile Sailing Master Dobbins had gone to Buffalo in search of cannon and ordnance for the fleet.

Early in May the two gunboats and the schooner were safely launched behind the sandbar. Noah Brown had the two brigs, *Niagara* and *Lawrence,* ready to be launched on 24 May. Lieutenant Perry did not wait for the ceremony. Commodore Chauncey had promised him command of a Marine party at the proposed attack on Fort George at the Lake Ontario end of the Niagara River. There was an urgency in the summons, when it came, that would not brook a day's delay, else Perry might miss the action. The attack was a success, and as a result of the victory the British and Canadians pulled back along the whole length of the Niagara River. Perry seized the opportunity to remove from the Black Rock Navy Yard at the Lake Erie end of the river all the navy ships that were bottled up there. There were five vessels in the harbor, including *Caledonia*, which had been cut out by Lieutenant Elliott. These Perry loaded with naval stores of every sort, and, with the help of two hundred soldiers and teams of oxen, dragged the vessels out of the swift current of the river and past the empty British fort on the farther shore.

Oliver Hazard Perry was down sick with a remittent fever in the cabin of *Caledonia* when the flotilla sailed into headwinds from Buffalo on 13 June. Though ill, he had need to rise and to command. A boat put out from the shore to warn him that a squadron, which included Britain's biggest vessels in commission, was hunting him. With deck cargoes hampering the guns, and his ships woefully undermanned, Lieutenant Perry was unprepared to fight his way home. He relied on the shallow draft of his vessels and the stormy west wind to avoid the British squadron. He was quicker than his enemy, and was safely behind the sandbar before the British came sniffing at the mouth of the Bay. The Americans had gone to ground. In the depth of Presque Isle Bay Lieutenant Perry, captain of a ship and commodore of the Lake Erie fleet, had all the war boats of his command. He had from Buffalo and Pittsburgh the materials to complete construction and go forth to battle. In June and early July Perry still lacked two elements of his command: men and freedom of movement. Trained sailors, competent aloft and experienced at gun drill, were scarce on the upper lakes, and the few sailors who came from the salt ocean were kept on Lake Ontario by Commodore Chauncey. The sandbar that gave the American shipyard protection from the big vessels from Canada was for Perry the security of a prison. Noah Brown's big brigs, *Lawrence* and *Niagara*, which constituted the American fleet's superiority over the British, could not sail out over the bar loaded down and ready to fight. The squadron from Fort Malden that followed Perry from Black Rock to Presque Isle Bay were like the wardens parading outside the door of a barred cell.

The British squadron did not loiter long off the mouth of the Bay. The British fleet had problems as great as those that plagued their Yankee enemy. When the 17-gun *Queen Charlotte, Hunter, Lady Prevost, Little Belt,* and *Chippewa,* returning from their cruise, dropped anchor in the Amherstburg roads they had a new captain commodore. The problems of the British fleet on Lake Erie in mid-June were the problems of Captain Robert Heriot Barclay, R.N. In the eight years since the battle of Trafalgar, Robert Barclay had almost become used to the empty sleeve that he wore pinned up as Horatio Nelson had done. He was twenty years old when he lost his arm on the day his great admiral died. He was twenty-eight, and a captain, on the day in June 1813 he came to Fort Malden to be commodore of the Lake Erie fleet. Barclay had come out to Canada the preceding autumn to command the fleet on Lake Ontario. But when Sir James Yeo, who had greater seniority, came out, Barclay had been sent to the west. As a "Captain," Barclay was under orders to

"General" Procter, as was the way of British service with combined amphibious command. In taking over his command under an army man, Captain Barclay, R.N., was also embarrassed by taking over ships and sailors traditionally belonging to an intensely inbred Provincial Marine. By his competence and his tact, Barclay overcame the aversion of the colonials for the Royal naval officer, and he got along with the difficult Procter although he had little influence on the general's plans. The obvious use of the British amphibious force in the spring of 1813 was in a strong army-navy attack on the American shipyard on Presque Isle Bay. A determined attack on the poorly defended base, and the destruction of the partly built American vessels, would assure the British naval supremacy for the year. But with Tecumseh at his shoulder and a horde of savages camping in his dooryard, Procter was compelled to use the volatile Indians in the easily accessible southwest corner of Lake Erie. Procter lay siege to Fort Meigs in May and, after Barclay had joined the fleet, chose to use only gunboats and transports for the limited objective attack on Fort Stephenson. Captain Barclay, with the capital ships of the British fleet, was off in the east, transporting stores, while Procter, with his troops and his Indian allies, was on the Sandusky.

The British at Malden were in need of the stores. Like his Yankee opposite number, Barclay needed many things for his new ship, *Detroit*, which when complete would give him near parity with the American fleet. General Procter needed supplies for his army, to carry out either a fighting role or a long retreat, the alternatives which had been given him by the governor general, whose favorite he was. There was an urgency to get those supplies to Malden. In May the

Americans had captured and burned York, the capital of Upper Canada on Ontario's north shore, and had severed, momentarily, the streets that linked Canada's east with the west. As Commodore Chauncey, U.S.N., held naval superiority over Commodore Yeo, R.N., the Americans were free to roam at will on Lake Ontario that early summer of 1813. The attack on York was followed by the successful American attack on Fort George, as a result of which the British and Canadians pulled back from the Niagara River line. Procter's army and navy were in danger of being cut off from the east. In that desperate case General Procter had orders to abandon the Detroit River holdings, retreat to the north, then move over the old portage route to the Ottawa River, and to add his force to the army at Montreal. For this long march he would need many supplies. The Royal navy on Lake Erie in July was the carrier for the army. Lack of seamen made any other role impractical. The sailors of the Provincial Marine were competent on the familiar lake, but they were too few. There were not enough of them to man the new *Detroit*. Perry, too, had an unmanned vessel, and both commodores on Lake Erie were begging their superiors for able seamen. Yeo was as reluctant as Chauncey to detach officers and men from Lake Ontario, and only a few made the overland journey from Kingston to Malden, or from Sackett's Harbor to Presque Isle.

Through all the drought of July, Captain Barclay kept his fleet on the lake, carrying, convoying, and keeping watch on the mouth of Presque Isle Bay. He could not go in over the sandbar, nor could Perry come out because of the extremely low water. At the very end of July, Captain Barclay lifted his blockade and sailed away. Rumor from Black Rock had it that

General Procter had concentrated troops at Long Point, directly across the lake, for a destructive raid on ⸀ resque Isle. The assumption was that Barclay had gone to fetch the troops. Panic seized the community on Presque Isle Bay. Civilians piled their goods on carts and set off for anywhere inland. On their way they met hurriedly assembled militia companies coming to the defense of the Bay. Major General David Mead was in command of the fifteen hundred Ohio militiamen who were uneasily setting up camp around the blockhouse and battery at the mouth of the Bay. When he arrived, the general had himself rowed out to the *Lawrence,* where he was met by a salute of cannon from the flagship. Perry met him on the quarterdeck and conducted his guest into the small cabin at the stern. While feet scuffed on the deck so close over their heads, Mead told of his plans for defense. Lieutenant Perry told the general of his plan to attack. The disappearance of Barclay from the mouth of the Bay was the opportunity Perry needed. All the activity on deck was in preparation for *Lawrence*'s lift over the sandbar. The salute for the general, in addition to being a courtesy, was to clear the guns which had to be off-loaded to lighten the brig. Fully manned or not, Perry must get his ships out onto Lake Erie. His fleet was useless and vulnerable in the bolthole of Presque Isle Bay.

On 1 August, Perry moved his fleet down to the mouth of the Bay and anchored behind the bar. The water was low and the channel so shallow that even the schooners had to be lightened to pass through. Some had doubts that the two brigs could ever pass over the bar and get through the channel. But Perry knew a method of crossing shallows, knowledge he had gained from the Dutch, who navigated much along the dunes of their North Sea coast. Perry first had *Lawrence* stripped of her guns, which were taken ashore and set upon the beach. Then the ballast rocks were taken out and piled. The brig floated high in the calm water. While this was going on he prepared two deep-hulled barges, called (from the Dutch) "camels." When these were ready and watertight he moved them into position on either side of *Lawrence* and had them filled with water. Then he ordered the barely floating camels lashed securely to the brig with slings and stayropes and spars, until *Lawrence* was a triple-hulled entity. When all was secure, Perry set as many men as he could get aboard the camels to bail them out. Sailors, sitting astride the barges' outer gunwales, dipped, lifted, and emptied their buckets overboard. As the weight of water was removed from the camels on either side of *Lawrence*, their increased buoyancy transmitted itself in part to the hull between them. Inch by inch, the brig's waterline rose above the level of the lake. Plank by plank, *Lawrence*'s hull came up, until the tall vessel seemed poised like a skimming bird. The camels, too, lay high and stolid on the water. Lieutenant Perry's careful calculations on paper had been correct. The deepest draft of the empty camels was less than the depth of the water over the sandbar. From the bow of *Lawrence*, Perry hailed the waiting towboats and helped secure them to his flagship and the camels. At his shout, the oars dug in and the sailors strained to move the mass of empty hulls all joined into one. Slowly the towboats moved forward to the chant of the boatswains. From their place in the stern, the captains of each could see the sandy bottom drop away into the deep water. *Lawrence* and the camels dutifully followed the towboats. At last she was safely over, the rowers slackened off, and *Lawrence* rode free on the threshold of the wide lake. The men refilled the camels with water, and Perry's flagship settled gently back into her element. As the camels were towed away, boats were coming alongside, bringing back the ballast rocks. The guns in their boats were crowding close behind, to be quickly hoisted aboard and hauled to their places on the brig's deck. Perry drove his men to get *Lawrence* ready again for action should the British come. But Barclay did not interrupt the delicate maneuver of the two brigs over the bar. He was far across the lake on business of his own.

By mid-afternoon of 4 August Perry was on the quarter-deck of his flagship, ready to defy the lake. The next day the camels carried *Niagara* safely over the shallows. At last, Commodore Perry of Lake Erie had his fleet on the inland sea.

XXV

"We Have Met the Enemy"

Oliver Hazard Perry sailed north. Behind the flagship the Lake Erie fleet of the United States navy held a ragged, uncertain line. The commodore had his vessels out for days on the shakedown cruise. On board *Lawrence* Perry had his crew up early and late at their exercises. Sticky blocks in the new brigs were freed; stays were tightened or loosened to give proper play to the masts. Ballast was shifted until the feel of the rudder was right under the steersman's hands. Stiff new rope became supple and lost its stretch with use and strain. Gun numbers practiced loading and running out the cannon. Powder boys found their way between the magazine and the guns they served. All hoped that along the hostile Canadian north shore, where they were cruising, a loaded coaster, Fort Malden-bound, would present a live target to give reality to the tedium of drill. On each vessel of Perry's fleet the captain studied his crew. With practice and improvements the bows that had wallowed and yawed began to lift to the press of sail above.

Decks became steady under the set of the captain's boot. Below decks the protesting groans of the newly joined timbers began to creak out the easy raucous song of a well-found ship under a sympathetic captain and crew. Commodore Perry sailed back to Presque Isle Bay on 9 August. The Lake Erie fleet, in a trim line astern of the flagship, responded smartly to the commodore's signal to anchor.

On shore, Lieutenant Jesse Elliott was waiting with a present for Perry: one hundred able-bodied seamen, with complementing junior officers. From the October night in 1812 when he cut out old *Detroit* and *Caledonia*, Jesse Elliott was the undoubted naval hero of Lake Erie. The appointment of an outsider to command did not dim the glory of Elliott's deed. Perry's seniority in rank did, however, place the local hero in a secondary position behind his unproven commander. That the notorious British Indian agent was a namesake and a relative was no more a valid charge against Elliott's loyalty than the fact that General William Hull and Isaac Hull, Captain of the U.S. frigate *Constitution*, had close relatives living in Canada. In Lieutenant Elliott, Commodore Perry had a second-in-command who knew Lake Erie and a naval officer to whom he could entrust his other capital vessel, *Niagara*. Elliott took command of that brig with the hundred seamen he had brought to the lake.

On 12 August Commodore Perry sailed west to report to General Harrison that the fleet was ready to begin operations. On the way, he diverted to look at Put-in-Bay, protected by the islands and islets of the Bass Island archipelago off the shore of Sandusky Point. Perry liked the harbor at Put-in-Bay. He found, too, that it was being watched by a British schooner, who also thought that it was a likely haven for the American fleet.

The following day Perry led the American squadron into Sandusky Bay, signaling with measured shot to coast watchers that he had come and that General Harrison was to be notified. A heavy rain was falling on the evening of 19 August, when William Henry Harrison arrived on the shore and saw the ten vessels of the American fleet anchored in the Bay. The general had brought with him from the Seneca Towns camp an imposing escort of soldiers. He had taken some pains to bring twenty-six chiefs with him, so that they might see for themselves the might of the United States upon the once British waters of Lake Erie.

General Harrison had himself rowed out to *Lawrence* in the rainy gloom of approaching night. He came aboard as the riding lights were being lit throughout the fleet. The red glow of the army's campfires could be seen ashore under the trees. That night the soldier and the sailor confirmed the timetable of future events, which each was confident he now controlled. The commodore would go out, find, fight, and defeat the British fleet. The general would complete the concentration of his forces on the peninsula forming Sandusky Bay and on the islands sheltering Put-in-Bay. Then together the fleet and the army would go to Fort Malden, where the soldiers would take the lead in conquering western Canada.

All day on 20 August, which was fine and clear, Perry and Harrison talked. They drew together in companionship as they sat in the stern of the commodore's boat on a pleasant sail out to see Put-in-Bay. They walked together, as the general pointed out campsites on the island, and the commodore talked of transports for the troops, and the supply line to be set up after the army had been landed on the Canadian shore. They took lunch together in the shade of a tree that overlooked the Bay, and looked to the line of the horizon, beyond which was Canada. The day after the sail to the islands, General Harrison returned to his camp at the Seneca Towns. Commodore Perry sailed with his fleet for Fort Malden.

Perry planned on doing battle with Barclay's fleet, less the new *Detroit*, in the mouth of the Detroit River. But that bold venture came to nothing. While he waited for the wind to change so that he could go in to attack, Perry was again taken with the old fever. The same fever flashed through the flagship like an explosion in the magazine. With *Lawrence* turned suddenly into a pest ship tended only by a bedridden doctor and a few convalescents, the whole fleet returned to Put-in-Bay. There Perry and the men recovered, and received aboard the fleet thirty-six soldiers sent by General Harrison to act as marines. Harrison had already sent to Perry a hundred seamen who had been found serving with the army as soldiers.

Though scarcely recovered and still weak, Perry set sail again for the Detroit River. But Barclay was safe under the guns of Fort Malden and would not be enticed out. The British commodore was waiting for more sailors, coming, he had been promised, from the Ontario fleet. With these he could man the new brig *Detroit*. Then he would have to go out with his fleet to fetch to Malden the supply boats, gathering at Long Point, which were so desperately needed.

Commodore Perry had grown restless, his restlessness had become impatience, and finally he could wait no longer. On the morrow the Americans would go in, as Nelson had at Aboukir Bay in Egypt, and fight the enemy at their anchorage. Perry's battle plan was dictated by his short-range hard-battering caronades. The American ships must sail in fast through the area where the British long guns could bear, and the Yankee caronades must remain silent. Once the Yankee captains were close alongside the British ships, their heavier weight of metal would pound the enemy hulls to pieces. Then, his policy reaffirmed, Perry assigned each of his captains an enemy vessel as his own to destroy.

Commodore Perry kept for himself the formidable *Detroit.* John Yarnall, first lieutenant on *Lawrence,* listened carefully to his captain and commodore, whose place on the quarterdeck he would take should Perry fall. The aloof and confident hero, Elliott, captain of *Niagara,* would attack *Queen Charlotte.* Daniel Turner, just out of his teens, and so newly commissioned lieutenant that he still wore his midshipman's coat, took the assignment for his 3-gun *Caledonia.* John Packet, as junior an officer as his friend on *Caledonia,* commanded the schooner-rigged *Ariel,* with her four squat 12-pound caronades. Commodore Perry's first cousin, Sailing Master Stephen Champlin, captained the 2-gun *Scorpion.* He was a rumpled old salt sailor at twenty-four. Thomas Almy was older, and, like Champlin, he had come to the lakes from the Newport gunboat squadron. He commanded *Somers.* August Concklin, George Senat, and Thomas Holdup, the orphan boy from South Carolina, each commanded a single gunboat, *Porcupine, Tigress, Trippe.* Only Sailing Master Dobbins was absent from Perry's fleet. In the schooner *Ohio,* he was on a voyage to Black Rock and Buffalo for supplies.

When the meeting was all but over Commodore Perry gave his officers the watchword for the battle. "Don't give up the ship." They were the words spoken by the dying captain of *Chesapeake* during the frigate's ill-fated duel off Boston. James Lawrence had died on *Chesapeake* in June, leaving his name for Perry's flagship and his dying words a motto for the U.S. navy. The purser of the Lake Erie fleet had had the sailmaker stitch a great square blue flag on which was written, in white letters a foot high, "Don't give up the ship." Perry displayed the flag to his captains and his officers on that night of 9 September. He told them that when that flag was hoisted to the masthead of *Lawrence*, it would be the signal to go in and engage. "If you lay your enemy close alongside, you cannot be out of place," Perry quoted Nelson in conclusion, then bade his officers good night. As they filed out he was carefully folding his battle flag.

The American fleet did not have to go in and get the British at their anchorage. In the morning of 10 September 1813, while Perry's men were making ready to sail for the Detroit River, the masthead lookout on *Lawrence* saw Barclay's fleet on the northwest horizon. One, two, three, four, five, six white sails were catching the slanting light of the rising sun. The lookout man sang out his news to the deck below. On all nine American vessels in Put-in-Bay the men paused in their work to hear the word. Their enemy was there. Arms pointed, faces turned to the northwest.

Commodore Barclay had at last received the long-promised crewmen from Lake Ontario. There were fewer men than he had asked for or expected, but enough to get the new *Detroit* under way with the other vessels. In all, Barclay had two hundred and thirty British and Canadian sailors, two hundred and forty British and Canadian soldiers loaned by Procter, and thirty-two good officers to command. Barclay was still under-manned at the guns and sails, and all his calculations gave him but two-thirds the over-all fighting strength of Perry's array. But the odds were Horatio Nelson's odds and Barclay took them with the utter confidence of his breed and service. Barclay had to go at once to Long Point to bring back the supply boats. Procter's soldiers, his sailors, and Tecumseh's Indians and their families at Fort Malden were eating twenty thousand rations a day. On 9 August Barclay dropped down to the mouth of the Detroit River with all his vessels. Early in the morning of 10 September he was underway in line of battle heading east into the rising sun.

The wind was from the southwest, favoring the British line, as the American ships worked their way out from among the islets and formed themselves into line of battle. A rain shower up out of Ohio passed over the American fleet and for a few short minutes obliterated from view the British fleet ten miles away. The storm passed. The sky and water were blue and sparkling, September-clear. Sailing Master William Taylor of *Lawrence* noted with relief that the wind had shifted to the southeast, and, though light, was holding steady from that quarter. He had been distressed when Commodore Perry had given him a course that would fetch him to leeward of the enemy. But Perry was determined to catch and fight the British that day, nor cared to whom was the advantage, so long as he laid his craft alongside Barclay's vessels.

Champlin and Packet in *Scorpion* and *Ariel* led the Ameri-can line, with *Lawrence* half a cable length behind the latter. *Caledonia*, an awkward sailer, followed next, but fell a little

behind her station. Elliott kept his quick, fast, and agile
Niagara a "half cable length" behind *Caledonia,* as ordered.
Somers and the three gunboats struggled to keep their place
and distance at the end of the line. After the rain passed Oliver
Hazard Perry had his first clear look at Barclay's squadron.
The British line was hove to, closed up, across the wind, bows
west. Perry's eyes were on the clean white sails of the 17-gun
Detroit, which he had chosen as his own. The schooner
Chippewa, one long 18, led the British line. *Detroit* was second,
with the brig *Hunter,* of 10 guns, next. Then came *Queen
Charlotte,* with 17 long guns; according to Perry's battle plan
she was Elliott's to fight. The 13-gun *Lady Prevost,* compli-
menting the wife of the governor general, and the sloop *Little
Belt,* 3 guns, completed Barclay's line. Perry, watching *Detroit,*
bore to cross that flagship's stern.

Now came the long haul into action, the interminable
minutes while the unhurried wind nudged the two fleets and a
thousand men along the collision course of battle. At ten
o'clock, Commodore Perry displayed his flag blazoned with
the motto "Don't give up the ship" to the crew of *Lawrence.*
He asked them if they would bide by the words and should he
fly it. The answer back was a loud "Aye! Aye!" and they
cheered when the blue and white flag broke out at the
mainmast head. Cheers from the vessels fore and aft established
the Americans' watchword in the hearts of the navy on Lake
Erie. It grew quiet on *Lawrence*'s deck. To break the anxious
stillness of the gun crews and the sailors crouching at their
battle stations, Perry ordered the mess captains to the galley to
bring up dinner. While the men ate, the cooks put out the fire
in the galley. Time hung heavily as the brig lumbered on. The

hulls of the British ships took form under the tall masts draped with the sails empty of the wind. Gun captains busied themselves at unnecessary tasks and set their gun numbers to do again things already done. Surgeon Parsons appeared head and shoulders out of the open deck hatch, looked around, caught a look from his fever patient Commodore Perry, and hurriedly descended again to the cockpit where his instruments were all laid out, his mates ready. It was the time when men remembered and worried. Somewhere in the long line of lashed hammocks filling the rack on top of the high gunwales was a clay pipe. Carefully wrapped in a blue handkerchief, with a twist of tobacco, the favorite thing was vulnerable to screaming shattering round shot. Perry set the men to wetting down and sanding the long expanse of scrubbed deck. The men, eager to be busy, sprang to the work. Aloft in the rigging, the Kentucky riflemen serving as marines re-tied the lines that would keep them from falling onto the crowded deck below. Looking down from the tops, the marines could pick out the casual figure of the officer who had recruited, drilled, and trained them into the prideful mysteries of The Corps. Everyone agreed that Lieutenant John Brooks was the finest looking of men. His impeccable dress and polished, courteous manners always endeared him to his men. Commodore Perry was impressive, though plainly dressed in a blue nankeen jacket. He walked the deck, talking and encouraging the waiting men. At the bow he took appraising glances at the enemy line, looming larger now but still beyond range of the long swiveled 32-pounder in *Scorpion*, two vessels ahead. From the stern Commodore Perry could see *Caledonia* dropping behind and Elliot in the capital ship *Niagara* doggedly keeping his station in the stretching line. Everywhere that Perry went, foreward, aft, below, his dog followed him. When *Lawrence* was a long country mile from the enemy, Perry had his dog taken below and secured in the pantry where the mess crockery was stored. Perry himself took station aft to await the first shot from the long guns of the British fleet.

The first shot came at a quarter to noon. It fell harmlessly into the water, short of *Lawrence*. Stephen Champlin tried his long 32 at the nearest enemy. It too fell short. Five minutes more of waiting and a British 24-pound shot crashed through the bulwarks of *Lawrence*. *Ariel*, just ahead, was firing, and Perry gave the order for the long 12-pounder in the bow to try for His Majesty's brig *Detroit*. Shots from the British flagship were striking regularly now on *Lawrence*, and the guns of the British *Hunter* were coming into range. The first of the American casualties, mostly wounded by splinters, were making their way toward the cockpit hatch. Perry and all his crew had to wait out their period of helplessness through the deadly zone where the long British guns could punish, and their own short carronades were useless iron monsters. A glance through the after gunport showed Perry that *Caledonia* had fallen behind. *Niagara* doggedly kept station half a cable length behind *Caledonia*. *Trippe*, the last of the struggling gunboats, coming up with all possible speed, was almost two miles away. A round shot struck high on *Lawrence*'s bulwarks aft and caromed off with the scream of a banshee in an Irish bog. A surprised grunt behind the commodore made him turn. Down on the deck, struck sideways by a shattered plank hurled from the broken bulwark, lay fourteen-year-old Alexander Perry. Instinctively, Oliver Hazard Perry turned from his ship to his brother. Slowly Alexander rose to his knees and struggled upright, pale, shaken, and hurt, to take his given place behind his commodore. *Lawrence* plowed on. She was approaching the smoke-shrouded British line at a sharp angle that would soon bring her broadside to bear on *Detroit.* Perry noted that *Queen Charlotte,* which Elliott should have been engaging, was moving slowly ahead to the point where *Lawrence* would meet the British line. In a matter of three minutes, Commodore Perry could give the order for the broadside. The flagship had been in the deadly zone for fifteen horrible minutes. Her rigging, as yet not too much damaged, still gave *Lawrence* headway. Barclay was aiming at the American's hull, guns, and crew. *Lawrence* was taking casualties on deck.

The gun captains and the division officers all along the starboard battery were looking aft to the quarterdeck, where Perry stood judging the moment. It came with a nod and a quiet order. The whole battery bellowed in unison, the guns lurched back into their retaining tracks with a rumble of wheels. The crew of *Lawrence,* the awful waiting over, leaped forward into action.

With his opening broadside Commodore Perry had done all he could for his fleet. *Scorpion* and *Ariel* were in action ahead, but they were drawing little fire from the British, who were concentrating on *Lawrence.* By flags and speaking trumpet, Perry had ordered the fleet astern to break line and engage at once. Perry had seen the order transmitted by *Caledonia* and Elliott on *Niagara.* Now, and for the next two hours, Commodore Perry was captain of a ship in close battle. Perry concentrated his own vessel's 10-gun broadside on the British flagship, aiming his heavy carronades on the enemy bulwarks.

When *Queen Charlotte* came up, passing *Hunter* to engage *Lawrence* at half a musketshot range, Perry still kept his guns on Barclay's new ship. *Detroit* was taking heavy punishment. Officer casualties were high. Though repeatedly injured and his one remaining arm wounded and helpless, Barclay himself still kept the deck. On board *Lawrence*, First Lieutenant Yarnall came aft to ask for other officers to command the guns still in action on the starboard battery. Perry gave him what he had left. The British *Hunter* was astern, in a position to rake with a 5-gun broadside. A bouncing round shot smashed the elegant Brooks's thigh, hurling him, writhing and screaming in agony, into the scuppers. They carried the marine into the cockpit and laid him down to die. Surgeon Parsons worked in the gloom below deck. Dying and dead lay in the dark corners. Less wounded men he patched in the light of the lantern and in that spot of September light that a penetrating round shot had let through the vessel's side. Powder boys ran up and down the aft companion ladder to and from the magazine. None heeded the captain's dog, whimpering amid the broken crockery littering the deck. A British round shot had penetrated to the dog's safe haven.

Lieutenant Yarnall, wounded, again came aft to ask for more officers and gun numbers. None were left. Perry himself was sighting a carronade. Yarnall went forward and, like his captain, sighted his own gun. Soon that, too, was out of action and he returned aft once more. The gun Perry was aiming had been hit and lay canted and useless on its broken carriage. After two hours of fighting, giving much, taking more, the guns of *Lawrence* were silent. Miraculously, Perry himself had not been touched. The blue and white flag still flapped at the masthead. Perry looked up. A gust of the increasing wind blew out the square burgee, revealing the motto, "Don't give up the ship." Perry ordered a boatswain to bring the flag to him. He sent his brother to bring a boat to the port gangway. Perry had decided to transfer with his flag to *Niagara* and bring that vessel into the fight. To Yarnall he gave the brave brig *Lawrence*, to hold out if he could or to surrender if he must. Perry went down into the boat, where Alexander and four seamen waited. At the moment of casting off, able bodied seaman Hosea Sargent pushed through the group at the head of the gangway. He had the blue and white burgee in a bundle in his hands. Perry reached and caught the bundle. The boat shoved off, the four sailors pulling on the oars, Alexander Perry clutching the tiller and giving the stroke, Oliver Hazard Perry standing in the stern, his back now to *Lawrence*, searching out *Niagara*.

In the freshening wind Elliott had at last forged ahead. He was passing *Caledonia*, who, her long 24-pounders blazing, was bearing down on *Hunter*. Perry saw that *Niagara*, all sails filled and drawing, was on a course that would pass the helpless *Lawrence* a quarter-mile upwind. Perry set his boat's course to intercept. He did not see the stars and stripes hauled down on *Lawrence*. The British fire, though only sporadic from *Detroit*, continued. Aboard the British flagship, Commodore Barclay was below, unconscious in his bunk. No other officer was on her deck, all having been severely wounded. Gun captains firing the remaining guns had switched their target from *Lawrence* to the bobbing little boat drawing away. They had guessed that the uniformed officer standing in the stern (Perry had changed into his dress coat) was important. Aboard *Queen*

Charlotte, small John Chapman, gunner, maintopman, and boarder, aimed a shot at the escaping Yankee commodore. It too missed the mark.

Jesse Elliott met his commodore on the deck of *Niagara* with a question as to how the battle went. Perry replied with a curt "Badly," and sent his second-in-command off in the boat to bring up the lumbering *Somers*, *Porcupine*, *Tigress*, and *Trippe*. With *Niagara*'s captain curtly dismissed, Perry, as captain as well as commodore, took command of the clean, tidy brig and its fresh crew. Up went the blue and white burgee to the masthead and with it soared the spirits of *Niagara*'s crew, so far denied the fight.

Beyond where *Lawrence* lay dead and tossing in the waves, Perry turned his new flagship toward the British line. He steered to cut across *Detroit*'s bows, going between her and *Lady Prevost*, which, during the two-hour fight, had moved ahead. As he passed through the enemy line he sent off broadsides, port and starboard. The port broadside cleared the decks of *Lady Prevost*'s crew. Only the dead remained above decks, along with their captain, holding his badly wounded face in bloody hands while he stared with glaze-shocked eyes at nothingness. *Niagara*'s starboard battery raked *Detroit* from stem to stern. Without officers, her crew disorganized, and her running gear damaged, the big ship fell off before the wind. She was out of control. In attempting to pass *Detroit* to get at *Niagara*, *Queen Charlotte*, still virtually undamaged, brushed the side of the British flagship. When Perry made his short turn to starboard beyond the British line he found the two enemy ships locked fast together in a hopeless tangle of rigging. Calmly, Perry backed his sails, and from over their bows sent

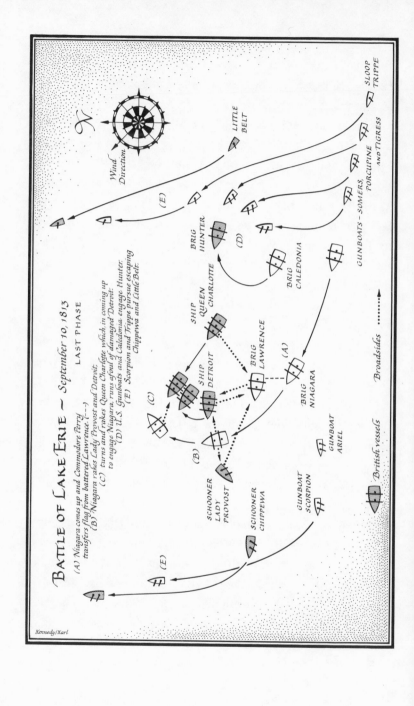

BATTLE OF LAKE ERIE ~ September 10, 1813

LAST PHASE

(A) Niagara comes up and Commodore Perry transfers flag from battered Lawrence. (→)
(B) Niagara rakes Lady Provost and Detroit.
(C) turns and rakes Queen Charlotte which, in coming up to engage Niagara, runs afoul of damaged Detroit.
(D) U.S. Gunboats and Caledonia engage Hunter.
(E) Scorpion and Tripp pursue escaping Chippewa and Little Belt.

Wind Direction

N

LITTLE BELT

(E)

BRIG HUNTER

(D)

BRIG CALEDONIA

SHIP QUEEN CHARLOTTE

SLOOP TRIPPE

GUNBOATS - SOMERS, PORCUPINE AND TIGRESS

SHIP DETROIT

BRIG LAWRENCE

(C)

(B)

(A)

BRIG NIAGARA

GUNBOAT ARIEL

SCHOONER LADY PROVOST

SCHOONER CHIPPEWA

GUNBOAT SCORPION

(E)

Broadsides ....

British vessels

Kennedy/Karl

broadside after broadside raking the decks of *Queen Charlotte* and *Detroit* from stem to stern. Barclay's ensign was hauled down in surrender. For eight minutes of killing punishment, *Queen Charlotte* took *Niagara*'s shot and cannister. Captain Finnis was dead. Someone else struck the colors on *Queen Charlotte*. Aboard *Lady Prevost*, a witless captain still stood alone upon his quarterdeck. A sailor ventured up, lowered *Lady Prevost*'s flag, and scurried below again. Beset all around by the gunboats, *Somers*, and Lieutenant Turner's *Caledonia*, *H.M.S. Hunter* held out for minutes, then surrendered. Of the six ships of the British fleet, only the little schooner *Chippewa* and the sloop *Little Belt* still flew the British naval ensign on Lake Erie. They were out of the fight, fleeing toward Fort Malden and home. Champlin in *Scorpion* and Holdup in *Trippe* were in pursuit and overtaking.

The guns of battle fell silent shortly after the hour of three. The day was ending before Commodore Perry brought the fleet back into Put-in-Bay. The Stars and Stripes hung proudly over the flags of Britain on the four big prizes at anchor in the quiet water. The harvest moon was bright in the sky when Holdup and Champlin brought *Chippewa* and *Little Belt* into harbor. Sailing Master Champlin dropped anchor under the stern of *Lawrence*. The battered flagship lay quietly at her anchorage, drenched in the glory of moonlight, aglow with the deeds of her brave day. There was a yellow light in the broken windows of the great cabin aft.

Oliver Hazard Perry had returned with his flag to his old ship *Lawrence* at the end of the battle. There he took the surrender from a wan procession of tattered British officers. He had made concerned enquiry as to Commodore Barclay's wounds. He had seen to the care of the wounded, his own and the British. He had watched the dead consigned to the deep. At long last, with a course set for Put-in-Bay, Commodore Perry sat down on the gritty deck with his back against the transom, put his head down, and slept.

Before he left *Niagara*, Perry had written the first report of the battle for General Harrison, waiting so anxiously on the outcome. He wrote the simple message on the back of an old letter, his desk the cocked beaver hat he had worn all day. "We have met the enemy and they are ours. Two ships, two brigs, one schooner & one sloop. Yours, with great respect and esteem, O. H. Perry."

XXVI

Star Rise and Star Fall

Not until 12 September did General Henry Procter give up
hope that Commodore Barclay and the British fleet would
return victorious to the anchorage of Amherstburg. Gunfire
was said to have been heard faintly from over the lake in the
early afternoon of 10 September. But no boat came that
evening to the Detroit River to tell the news of victory or
defeat. There was no word on the eleventh or twelfth that
anyone anywhere on the Canadian coast had seen so much as a
distant topsail of Barclay's fleet. Six ships of the British navy
and all who sailed in them had disappeared over the horizon.
On 12 September General Procter wrote to General De
Rottenberg, Commander of all Upper Canada and therefore
next over Procter, that the British navy on Lake Erie was
probably lost. Procter's letter, and subsequent ones that he sent
pelting east, hinted that he would welcome orders from De
Rottenberg and the governor general himself to abandon all
western Canada and return with his soldiers to the bosom of
the army in the east or center. In anticipation of such an order,

previously talked of, Procter began a surreptitious movement
of stores from Fort Malden to Sandwich, the first short step on
the road east.

To the soldiers of the 41st Foot, going about their daily
business around the town and fort, General Procter kept up a
bold and cheerful front. Their two hundred and fifty comrades, gone with the fleet, would be back in good time, with
tall tales to tell. He saw a wagon train loaded with rations off
up the river road to Sandwich. More food for the winter would
be coming from Long Point with the fleet. He sent some boats
with military stores, accompanied by thin excuses, to that corner of Lake St. Clair where the River Thames ends its long
meander, a second step on the road east.

Procter avoided and ignored Tecumseh those first days after
Barclay's fleet was lost, while he yet vacillated and procrasti-
nated in making the decision of whether to stay and fight or to
run away. For the third time since spring, the Shawnee leader
had rallied warriors to go with the British to win back their
homeland from the Americans. Fifteen hundred Indian warriors were waiting Procter's lead. Their wives and children were
daily at the storehouses, demanding their rations. Any retreat
from the Detroit River was an abandonment of the Indians and
a repudiation of Tecumseh's dream of a united Indian
federation in the American Northwest. Procter could not, for
long, keep the secret of Barclay's whereabouts, now known,
from the wise Indian. Nor could he keep secret from the
contemptuous Tecumseh his intention to run. On 18 September, the eighth day after the fleet was lost, Tecumseh
confronted Procter in a conference held in a nearly empty
storehouse. Tecumseh had all his chiefs with him. The

credulity of the Indians had snapped like a cut bowstring that morning, when they heard that Procter had ordered the evacuation of Detroit and the destruction of all His Majesty's property in the town.

Tecumseh, imposing as always in his pale doeskin dress, spared the young British general nothing. With the sharp edge of the oratory Tecumseh used so well, he reminded Procter of all the promises he had broken. He demanded the promised arms and in return he pledged that the Indians, shouting their approval into the rafters of the hollow shed, would win back their hunting ground or leave their bones upon the land. Twisting the cutting words with a skilled thrust, Tecumseh called Henry Procter a "fat dog" who "drops its tail between its legs and runs off."

With an Indian problem now added to his woes, Procter again put off making the decision to retreat. No one came forward to help the general make up his mind. Finally, as time ran out, Tecumseh, his rage cooled, consented to accompany Procter to Moravian Town, about thirty-five miles up the Thames River as the wild duck flies. Near that wretched little village, named for its mission, Procter promised to stand and fight.

On 24 September, Procter, his eight hundred regulars, and all the Indians, men, women, and children, were at Sandwich. Detroit, across the river, was evacuated of all things British. Fort Malden, the barracks, the shipyard that had built *H.M.S. Detroit,* all were smoldering ruins. On 26 September Yankee vessels were sighted at the mouth of the Detroit River. Only then did Procter order the withdrawal from Sandwich to the Thames River. The march-off began late the following day, with little haste and no urgency. Twenty-four hours later General William Henry Harrison landed with the American invasion army, three miles below Amherstburg.

On receiving Commodore Perry's eloquently simple note, William Henry Harrison had no doubts as to what he would do. Like a good teamster, he was ready to start at first light, with a well-greased wagon to drive behind a sleek team, eager to draw into supple harness. All summer, while he waited for the naval decision on the lake, General Harrison had been assembling his vehicle for invasion. Common prudence dictated that the American army stand on the defensive until the lake was won. Harrison, however, had contrived a poised defense that only required him to gather the reins together, give a flick of the whip, and with a "gee" lunge forward into the offense.

With only three thousand of the authorized seven thousand regulars trained and under arms, Harrison called on his old friend Governor Shelby for the Kentuckians who always fought so well under the hero of Tippecanoe. Governor Shelby came to the assembly point with two thousand men. He himself would lead his Kentuckians. Johnson's steel-hard mounted riflemen were back under Harrison's command, their order to go west having been countermanded by Washington City. Harrison had them standing by and grazing their horses in the corn around Fórt Meigs. When the time came they would ride north across the Raisin River to Detroit, to a rendezvous with Harrison's troops coming by boat from across the lake. Brigadier General Duncan McArthur, then commanding at Fort Meigs, was going on his second invasion of Canada across the Detroit. Under Harrison, he would have a chance to show those qualities of loyalty that had been so markedly absent the year before, when he served under Hull. In mid-September McArthur brought his regulars in their bateaux from Maumee Bay to the assembly on the lower Portage River. He brought with him from Fort Meigs the Kentuckians of Green Clay's command, who, though their enlistment time was running out, wanted to follow Harrison to the end. Brigadier General Lewis Cass, the other dissident Ohio colonel under Hull, was there waiting with his brigade when McArthur arrived. With Harrison's invasion army were two hundred and fifty Indians, a token that the old treaties with the nations were valid treaties. Their presence among the bluecoated soldiers was mute acknowledgment that the White Father in Washington City was strong and victorious and would prove generous.

Off the Ohio coast, in Put-in-Bay, Commodore Perry had set his fleet in order. Rigging had been spliced, sails patched, and new planks fitted into hulls and bulwarks of both the American ships and the prizes. Sailors on their knees had rubbed hard to obliterate the dark stains of blood from the white planking of the decks. The fleet was ready on 20 September. On 24 and 25 September the troops were ferried in fine weather from the mainland to the islands. On the morning of 27 September the last of five thousand soldiers found their assigned places on the sixteen armed vessels and a hundred other craft. The weather was fair, the lake gentle, and again the wind from the southwest favored Perry and his course for the mouth of the Detroit River. General Harrison issued his general order, calling his soldiers "sons of sires whose fame is immortal." He reminded his Kentuckians of the River

Raisin and cautioned the wild frontiersmen against reprisal after victory. The sails were filling to the wind. The invasion of Canada was under way.

At four o'clock the landing force touched down on the low sandy beach at Hartley's Point, inside the mouth of the river. The soldiers came ashore, running and splashing through the shallows. They deployed quickly, and still running, gained the high drifts beyond the beach. No enemy was there, only the waving sand grass. Scouts went inland to the coast road. Still no enemy. On the beach General Harrison was hurrying the men into their companies and on their way to the road that led to Amherstburg. Governor Shelby was on the road, assembling the advance guard. They were still falling into columns when the old governor strode out on the three-mile walk to town. He was still setting the pace for the youngest rifleman when he came to the first house of the town. Shelby doffed his hat to the group of ladies waiting there to receive him. He stood with them, assuring them of mercy and protection as his riflemen marched on into Amherstburg. Beyond, columns of smoke were rising from the charred ruins of Fort Malden.

Harrison had expected to get horses at Amherstburg to replace those that had been left behind for lack of transport space. But in his flight Procter had taken all but a single Canadian pony. Harrison gave this sorry mount to the grateful old Governor Shelby. Colonel Ball, with his dismounted Dragoons, had gone ahead to secure the bridge over the Aux Canards River. They did this, beating off the rear guard of Procter's regulars in the process. Marching across the once-contested bridge, many of Harrison's men were on familiar ground. They marched on past the old Mission Church at

Sandwich, saw the old stone mill, and turned off to camp by
Colonel Babee's fine house, where General Hull had made his
first headquarters on Canadian soil. Across the broad river
were the houses of Detroit. General McArthur had crossed
over with seven hundred men and secured the town under the
Stars and Stripes. On the river the American fleet rode, bows
set into the flow out of Lake Huron and the lakes beyond.
Colonel Richard Johnson and his mounted Kentucky riflemen
rode into Detroit the next day, 30 September, and tethered
their mounts on the river shore, ready to be transported into
Canada.

General Harrison had written from Amherstburg to the
Secretary of War that because Procter had so many horses he
would set a hard pace for the American pursuers to overcome.
But Procter was a slow man, hampered by indecisions. A
squadron from Perry's fleet almost caught up with the British
supply boats before they could duck into the Thames River,
like woodchucks into a dry stone wall.

The American army, less McArthur's contingent at Detroit,
began the pursuit of Procter on 2 October. Seven British
deserters, anxious to talk, gave Harrison news of his quarry.
Procter was only fifteen miles up the River Thames, on the
right bank. He had seven hundred regulars in his army. There
were no Canadian militia, the men having been sent home to
bring in the harvest. Of Tecumseh's Indians, perhaps twelve
hundred remained with the Shawnee. The Indians lost interest
in war when called on to march backwards.

Encouraged by the nearness of the enemy, Harrison pressed
the pursuit. He marched up the left bank of the river, winding
its way up the fruitful valley. At Drake's farm he left *Scorpion,*

Tigress, and *Porcupine,* which had accompanied the army.
Beyond the farm the riverbanks were high and the open decks
of the boats were vulnerable. Harrison did not leave all the
navy there. Commodore Perry in his marching boots had
joined General Cass as a volunteer aide.

Beyond Drake's farm lay Dolsen's riverside farm, where
Procter had meant to make his stand. Harrison did not know
that Procter had left the army for three days to take his wife
and his ailing daughter to the mission at Moravian Town.
Lieutenant Colonel Augustus Warburton of the 41st was
conducting the retreat, and he had left Dolsen's behind. On 4
October, when Procter rejoined his miserable, disheartened
force, the Americans were finding fresh spoor of the British
army. Johnson's mounted men had two sharp skirmishes with
Indians. They were the Indians who still wanted to fight for
Tecumseh's dream, not like old Walk-in-the-Water, who,
with sixty warriors, had given himself up earlier that morning.
McGregor's mill and its store of wheat were still burning
furiously when the marching army came up to it. They had to
walk wide around the pyre. A detachment of cavalry, by
galloping across the neck of a horseshoe bend of the river,
surprised an ammunition boat before it could be burned. Two
burning boats were found above the first. They were drawn
into the bank at Bowle's farm, five miles above the town of
Chatham. Harrison ordered the army to halt for the night at
the farm. The soldiers, dismissed from the march, gathered to
watch a near by distillery burn down. They did not know
until the flames died down that the distillery had been a store
for the Canadian militia's arms.

On the morning of 5 October Johnson's men captured two

ammunition boats intact and several bateaux with their crews. Mid-morning found Harrison at Arnold's mill, the last ford across the Thames before Moravian Town. General Harrison decided to cross the river there. Eight miles up the north bank, Johnson's cavalry halted until Harrison and the infantry came up. Johnson showed his general the campsite where Procter's army had stayed the night before. Here were the tent pegs of an officer's tent, there the ashes of Indians' small fires. All around was the cast away debris of many men who had departed quickly. Colonel Johnson's prize exhibit was a wagon driver, caught within the hour, who said that the main British force was in battle array across the road, "Just yonder a piece."

Henry Procter had left his traveling carriage well to the rear of his battle line. But not too far away to be handy. His one cannon was placed in the middle of the road, aiming back at Detroit, Amherstburg, and all the places he had abandoned. Between the road and a small marsh, the regulars were drawn up in two rows. They faced west into a wood of well-spaced hardwood trees. There was scarcely any underbrush for the distance of a short musketshot. On the north side of the little marsh was a narrow corridor of firm ground beyond which the tangle of a large swamp delineated the whole right flank of Procter's chosen battleground. A small group of regulars held the narrow corridor, with Tecumseh's Indians supporting them. Tecumseh himself was there, standing near the edge of the marsh. From this vantage point he was close enough to co-ordinate his half of the field with Procter's. The two commanders had talked. Tecumseh pointed out that most of his Indians were in firing positions along the edge of the swamp. The Indians under Oshawahnah were in echelon forward, making the long side of a letter "L" with their British brothers. The position was a classic ambush. Before he left the British general, so pale a shadow of the mighty Isaac Brock, Tecumseh, the Shooting Star, made his peace with young Henry Procter. The allies shook hands and Tecumseh returned to make his stand. Procter stayed behind his second line.

General Harrison, advancing behind Colonel Johnson's mounted riflemen, had planned to attack by passing his foot soldiers in two divisions through the cavalry, who would be used, properly, in pursuit. The American left division would guard the flank against the swamp, where, remembering Fallen Timbers, he knew the Indians would be sure to lie in ambush. The right division of Americans would attack the solid wall of British regulars they expected to find ahead. Governor Shelby commanded from a position where the two divisions joined, inland of the small marsh. General Harrison, with Brigadier Cass, Commodore Perry, and the officer Gallopers of his staff, marched down the road. All of Harrison's men were Kentuckians. The hundred and twenty soldiers of the 27th Infantry, the only regulars with him, had been given a special duty. They were to attack and capture Procter's single field gun. Forty Indians went with the regulars, sneaking forward under the bank of the river. All was carefully planned for the American attack.

Then, at the moment when the American infantry should have gone forward, William Henry Harrison changed his plans. A scout reported that the British were not in mass, but were stretched across the forest floor in two extended and separated lines. Harrison knew how Kentucky mounted men attacked, weaving their agile ponies through brush, leaping windfalls, firing with effect with rifle or pistol from horseback, and hollering to scare the squirrels out of the trees. The general gave the attack on the British regulars to his friend Colonel Richard Johnson. That officer quickly formed his riflemen into six columns. Four would charge between the marsh and the river. Lieutenant Colonel James Johnson commanded this wing. He rode on slowly, picking his way through the underbrush, toward the park-like part of the wood where the enemy stood waiting. James Johnson's two sons rode behind him. Looking back, the boys saw their uncle, their colonel, ride away into the marsh, two columns of horse wheeling left to follow. He was going to attack in the corridor beyond the marsh. The two boys, riding stirrup to stirrup, came behind their father out of the thick growth into the parkland. Ahead of them a long ragged line of redcoated soldiers, stood looking at them over leveled muskets tipped with shining bayonets. A shouted order, "Fire!" and the British line turned into billowing smoke. Cut leaves floated down, shot whirred by the Kentuckians' heads, and the sound of muskets discharged rolled over the mounted columns. One horse was kicking, others danced or stood stock still, trembling, as the riders soothed and regained control of their startled beasts. Up ahead, the redcoated line was methodically going through the drill of reloading. The Kentuckians kicked the flanks of their mounts, someone shouted, "Remember the River Raisin" and the four columns of horsemen surged forward. The second British volley did not stop the mad, shouting gallop. Scattered as they were, the British regulars could not form the squares that were their only defense against a cavalry charge. James Johnson's men rode in among the foot soldiers, bowling them over, clubbing them with rifles and pistols. The British regulars threw down their muskets and surrendered. The charge of the mounted riflemen carried them through the single volley of the second British line, which likewise surrendered. Some, near the marsh, ran away. On the Kentuckians' right the British cannon was silent, taken before it could fire a shot. The soldiers of the 27th cheered the horsemen as they careered past.

There was much shooting beyond the marsh. The regulars with their capture gun, and the prisoners of James Johnson's charge under guard, could only listen and read the course of the battle there. Between the marsh and the big swamp, the brush was thicker than it was on the roadside. Most of Richard Johnson's men dismounted to stride on through, their rifles high and ready, as for wing-shooting of the thunderous grouse. Colonel Johnson, with his close friends who called themselves "The Forlorn Hope," rode forward close to the edge of the marsh. On the left their men were engaged, and the musketfire was falling back before the sharper crack of the rifles. Johnson was riding a white pony, his servant's mount, his own having gone lame that morning. Without warning a volley at short range surprised The Forlorn Hope. William Whiteley, seventy years old, was shot dead. Johnson was hit in his thigh and hip. The wound was not enough to unhorse him or stop him from kicking the little horse into a gallop toward an Indian in pale buckskin, leveling a pistol at him. The Indian fired. The bullet raked Johnson's arm from hand to elbow. Johnson fired his pistol at close range and the shot struck the Indian in the face, sending him backwards, sprawling, dead. The Indians had gone as quickly as they had come. The Forlorn Hope plunged on into the thicket. Samuel Theobald of Johnson's staff held back, seeing that his colonel was wounded and bleeding. Quietly he took the bridle of the white pony and led it gently back through the marsh in search of a surgeon. The battle carried on toward the east and there the firing stopped, marking the sudden end of a battle scarcely ten minutes old. No enemy was left fighting in the field. Oshawahnah's Indians on the flank had slipped away to where their women and children waited. For them the long road of wandering in search of a peaceful home had only begun.

General Procter was not among the prisoners sitting dejectedly on the side of the road by the brass cannon. Procter had gone. He was not heard of until after dark on that night of 5 October 1813. Then General Procter's fine light carriage drove up, side lamps lit, with Major E. D. Wood on the driver's box. The major had come upon the abandoned carriage well beyond Moravian Town. On the back seat lay General Procter's cocked hat and his sword in its scabbard. The general himself was far away and going farther when the mounted riflemen came up to the carriage.

Tecumseh, too, was gone. No one ever knew where. One dying British soldier, a man named Clarke, who had been an Indian interpreter for Procter, told Captain Benjamin Warfield of Johnson's regiment that the great Indian leader was dead. Clarke had seen the body carried away to be buried with proper lamentations in some secret place. The rumor went through the American army that Colonel Richard Johnson had been wounded by Tecumseh himself and that the Indian in pale buckskin whom the Kentuckian had shot in turn was the

Shawnee chief. The rumor was so strong that, in the morning, Samuel Theobald went back to the place where The Forlorn Hope had had its skirmish. Whiteley's body was there where the old man had fallen. The bodies of two Indians lay near by. They had been stripped naked. The older one, believed to be Tecumseh, had the skin flayed in strips from the thighs. Kentucky men found Indian leather a good souvenir when made into strops for their steel razors. Theobald had found among the prisoners a halfbreed named Anthony Shane, who claimed to have known Tecumseh. But when he was brought to view the mutilated body the Irish Indian could see no resemblance to his friend. Shane could have been lying. Clarke, now dead of his wound, could have been telling the truth. Colonel Johnson, on his way down the Thames to a long convalescence, could have shot Tecumseh dead. A third Indian could have been killed in the skirmish with The Forlorn Hope. Johnson would never say.

General William Henry Harrison believed only that the greatest of red men was dead. The man that he had faced in battle at Fallen Timbers, when both were young, was gone from the scene of war. The Indian leader whom Governor Harrison had confronted beneath the council tree at *Grouseland* on the far away Wabash was no longer an enemy to meet anywhere. The long battle between the two strong men of opposed ideas was over. The white man at last held the homeland for which both had fought so long and so hard. The red man's hopes had finally set with the westering sun. Harrison's bright star was high in the firmament of the Northwest and rising higher. Tecumseh, the Shooting Star, had fallen to earth.

Afterword

In his camp by the Thames near Moravian Town General William Henry Harrison read the reports of the casualties of his latest and last battle. They were light: twelve British, twelve Americans killed, and thirty-three Indian bodies found. There was little booty from the fast-fleeing, light-traveling British army of the west: the field gun taken by the regulars on the road, eight or ten other cannon found abandoned above Moravian Town, several wagons, and Procter's carriage. In a wagon were found most of the American flags and regimental standards captured from General Hull's and Winchester's sorry defeats and Colonel Dudley's bold but blundering charge. Only the color of the 4th Regiment of Infantry, surrendered at Detroit, was missing from the bundle. Gone, too, was the King's color. The regimental color of the 41st Foot was not there, but even though he did not have the trophies, Harrison had four hundred and seventy-seven soldiers of that regiment to send to Ohio to join their two hundred and fifty comrades captured with Barclay's fleet.

On the second day after the battle General Harrison returned to Detroit, riding along with the horsemen of Colonel Johnson's regiment. Governor Shelby followed the road back with the foot soldiers. The American general did not choose to continue his drive up the Thames, although that route led straight to the right rear of the British army, holding desperately to the Niagara front. Dundas Street as a road had not been able to supply Procter, and Harrison knew that it could not hold up under the march of the Americans or the passage of the supply wagons. The safe way, the sure way, to aid the American army fighting on the Niagara line was by the lake which Perry had so decisively won. General Harrison would go to Niagara later, but first he had work to do in the restored Territory of Michigan and elsewhere in the Eighth Military District, which he commanded.

During the fourteen years between his resignation as a captain in the old 1st Infantry and his recommissioning as a brigadier general, William Henry Harrison had dealt with Indians. He had attended conferences and made treaties with the nations of the Northwest. He had been gentle with the former war chief of the Miami, Little Turtle. He had been firm and unafraid when Tecumseh faced him with unnegotiable demands. Harrison had been harsh toward the mad Prophet and his bewitched followers on Tippecanoe Creek. Now, in October 1813, with the British discredited before the Indian nations, Major General Harrison was ready to offer to the nations peace and the hand of friendship under amnesty. Many chiefs had come in and received assurance before the Battle of the Thames. In October, Oshawahnah, the chief who had fought on with the British, came to Detroit asking forgiveness.

On 14 October an armistice was signed preparatory to the holding of a future council of peace. With an amnesty of the United States government secured, the Indians left to face the oncoming winter. The Americans at Detroit were glad to see the Indians go away. They had provided for over three thousand hungry red guests since the British had gone from the Detroit River. Brigadier General Lewis Cass, officer commanding and temporary governor of Michigan, had his thousand troops and his civilians to provender and care for through the coming winter. October signs indicated that the winter at Detroit would be hard for the people and difficult for those in authority.

Even before General Harrison left with McArthur's brigade for the Niagara front, the weather had halted further fighting in the Northwest. A naval expedition to recapture Mackinac was called off. That last British fort could wait until spring, as could the more distant Indians in the north and far west who still listened to the British Indian agents there.

But when spring came the American effort was dilatory. Mackinac did not fall. For want of energy, Perry's ships failed to stop the Northeast Company's furs from Lake Superior from reaching Montreal. They were taken by way of the portage from Georgian Bay to the Ottawa River. The Indians along the upper Mississippi raided under British aegis as they had in the early days of war along the Ohio. The old 1st Infantry was there, fighting lonely skirmishes as they had always done. In the white man's land of the Northwest, where territories had become states or near states, the peace was being established. The old hero of the Northwest was back in civilian clothes, consolidating what his efforts had earned.

William Henry Harrison had gone east to fight the British. The war for the Northwest that gave the land between the Ohio and the Great Lakes to the United States had been a long one. It had truly begun when General Harmar with the First United States Regiment had marched north in 1790. It did not end until twenty-three years later, when General Harrison returned from the River Thames, leaving on Canadian soil the body and the spirit of Tecumseh, the Shawnee.

Postscript on Careers

William Henry Harrison served briefly on the Niagara front during the late fall and early winter of 1813 and 1814. His relations with Secretary of War Armstrong had always been strained, mainly because of Armstrong's direct interference in Harrison's command, such as his arbitrary assignment of Johnson's regiment to the Far West before Procter's attack on Sandusky. When Harrison, on leave in Cincinnati, received no assignment for the 1814 season, he sent in his letter of resignation from the army. His resignation was promptly accepted by Secretary Armstrong, who did not wait to consult with President Madison, then absent from the capital. When the President returned, he immediately appointed Harrison to the commission to settle Indian affairs in the Northwest. At a second treaty of Greenville, held in July 1814, the Indians agreed to take up arms with the Americans should the British attack United States territory. As a result of this treaty the British peace commissioners, meeting in Ghent, abandoned their former allies. A further Indian conference at Detroit in

1815 settled future territorial relations between the Indian nations and ended Harrison's direct negotiations with the Indians.

William Henry Harrison went into politics in 1816, being sent that year to the House of Representatives, where he remained until 1819. After service in the Ohio Senate, during which time he supported Henry Clay's unsuccessful bid for the presidency in 1824, Harrison served in the United States Senate from 1825 to 1828. His political career was active without being distinguished. He had friends who continued to support him, but his opposition to Andrew Jackson, the final hero of the War of 1812, cost him the command of the army and ended a brief tour as United States Minister to the South American Republic of Colombia. Harrison's friends continued to push him forward. He was defeated by Henry Clay for the Democratic/Republican party nomination for President in 1832. As the Whig party candidate for President in 1836, Harrison was trounced by Democratic Martin Van Buren. In 1840 "Old Tippecanoe" Harrison won the presidency from Van Buren with a "Log Cabin and Hard Cider" campaign. But the old soldier lived only a month longer. President William Henry Harrison died in office on 4 April 1841.

Zachary Taylor defeated Winfield Scott, also an 1812 and Mexican War figure, for the Whig party nomination for President in the 1848 election. Taylor won the election from Lewis Cass, sometime colonel of Ohio militia under William Hull. President Taylor died in office 9 July 1850, at sixty-six years of age.

Colonel Richard Mentor Johnson was a part-time soldier during 1812 and 1813. He was born in 1780, and in 1807 he was a member of the United States Congress from Tennessee. However, he chose to represent his constituents from the saddle rather than in his seat in the House. He raised and led his regiment of Kentucky mounted riflemen and fought hard and boldly under Harrison. Johnson's charge on 5 October 1813 was the Battle of the Thames. He recovered from the multiple wounds he received in that battle and returned to serve in the House of Representatives until sent to the Senate. Johnson's political career peaked in the presidential campaign of 1837 when, as Martin Van Buren's running mate, he became Vice President. After his term in office he retired to an active life in Kentucky, where he died at the age of seventy in 1850.

Lewis Cass, born in New Hampshire, had been a troublesome subordinate to the unfortunate Hull in 1812, and continued this role through a long political career which never achieved the success for which he strove. As governor of Michigan Territory from 1813 to 1831, Cass did much solid work in councils and in formulating treaties with the Indians. He entered national politics as President Jackson's Secretary of War in 1831, and in 1836 Jackson appointed Cass Minister to France. Cass returned from abroad to serve in the United States Senate, from which position he made strong bids for the Democratic candidacy for the presidency in 1844 and in 1852. He refused the nomination in 1856. The high point in Cass's career was in 1848, when he ran against General Taylor for the presidency of the United States.

Colonel Duncan McArthur served in Congress and later as governor of Ohio.

Robert Lucas, who resigned a brigadier general's commission to be a captain in the United States Army, had the unusual distinction of serving as governor of both Ohio and, later, Iowa.

The rise of state militia officers to high office was not remarkable, as their initial appointment to militia rank was made because of their civic and political activities and abilities. Thus, at war's end, most militia officers returned to public life to become judges and legislators, and to continue active careers in their states, counties, or communities.

Oliver Hazard Perry's subsequent career was short-lived. After the War of 1812, he commanded frigates of the United States Navy as a post captain until his premature death in 1819, at the age of thirty-four, while commanding a squadron in the West Indies. Perry's death shocked the nation, which had adored him as the epitome of its pride in its navy. In 1826 Perry's body was brought home to a funeral that demonstrated the nation's grief.

Of the enemy, General Isaac Brock, who was killed in battle shortly after his incisive capture of Detroit, is, with Montcalm, James Wolfe, and "Billy" Bishop, one of the military heroes of Canada.

General Henry Procter, the anti-hero of the war in the

Northwest, was court-martialed, rebuked, and allowed to return to England, where he died in the late 1850's.

For Tecumseh, killed in the final battle of the war for the West which he waged during all his life, was reserved the admiration and respect of his former deadly enemies. The United States Navy, which often names its vessels after great Americans, had its "Tecumseh." The figurehead of that ship is the visual emblem of the United States Naval Academy, and the Shawnee chief is invoked by midshipmen for victory and success.

Black Hawk, a Sauk chief, fell heir to Tecumseh's dream of a United Nations of Indians. He had followed and fought at the side of the Shawnee leader in Ohio and Michigan and in Canada at the Battle of the Thames. Black Hawk carried the struggle and the war further west. His efforts culminated in a short war fought in western Illinois and Wisconsin. "The Black Hawk War" is unusual in that it bears the name of a man.

The Beginnings of the United States Army

By June 1784 General George Washington's "Continentals," soldiers raised and provided for by the Continental Congress, were disbanded. Largely by the devotion and efforts of those soldiers, the American War of Independence was won and the government of the thirteen rebellious colonies, united in the Continental Congress, was preserved. With the threat and menace over, the Continental Congress disbanded the Continentals, as "standing armies in time of peace are inconsistent with the principles of republican government, dangerous to the liberties of a free people, and generally converted into destructive engines for establishing despotism. . . ."

A thin thread of army blue did remain to link the old Continentals to the new army, which, in spite of a reluctant Congress, was inevitably created. By the above quoted act of the Continental Congress (2 June 1784), 80 privates of an artillery company were retained to "guard stores" at West Point on the Hudson and at Fort Pitt on the Ohio. Their commanding

262

officer, and therefore the commanding officer of the army, was a captain.

Circumstances of Indian unrest in the West soon drove the Continental Congress to increase the army of caretakers to a force of 700 men who, except for those at West Point, manned forts west of the Allegheny Mountains. Lieutenant Colonel Josiah Harmar commanded these men. Harmar continued in actual command under the Continental Congress, which had direct management of the army. When the Constitution came into effect, on 30 April 1789 it created a new, federal, government, and it designated the President, George Washington, Commander in Chief of the Army.

Before the Constitution was signed, as at the time of Shays's Rebellion in Massachusetts in 1786, threats to the security of the new nation were met by congressional callups of state militiamen. That system was again used when, in 1790, it was decided to send a punitive expedition against the British-agitated Indians on the Maumee River. Militiamen from four states were called up for the summer months into the "service of the United States." Ninety "regulars" of the Regiment of Infantry culled from the garrisons of western forts were added to the force which was given to Lt. Col. Harmar. The utter defeat of this untrained army of men under short-term enlistment led to the expansion of the regular army, still doing garrison and caretaker work in the West. By an Act of Congress dated 3 March 1791 a 2nd Regiment of Infantry (the old regiment became the 1st) was authorized, as was a high command staff with a major general. The new organization, which included artillery specialists, was still ineffectual when Major General

Arthur St. Clair led the men out, in October 1791, on a second
punitive expedition. A second defeat resulted, in which soldiers
of the 1st and 2nd Infantry and the "Battalion of Artillery"
were involved.

A complete reorganization of the army, now recognized as a
necessity for the developing West, was effected in the year following St. Clair's defeat. With President Washington giving
the lead, the army (still a byword) was organized into the "Legion of the United States." The Legion was divided into four
sub-legions of approximately regimental strength; each consisted of infantry, riflemen, artillery, and dragoons. Command
was given to Major General Anthony Wayne. By inculcating
spirit and training into the sub-legions, this officer gave the
army cohesion. After two years' painstaking work, Wayne
was ready to employ his newly forged weapon at Fallen Timbers at the rapids of the Maumee River. The Legion won its
battle and gave to the Army of the United States a tradition of
victory.

The Legion organization ended in November 1796, when
separate arms of the service were re-formed. The four sub-legions became the 1st, 2nd, 3rd and 4th Regiments of Infantry.
Only two of the four troops of Legion cavalry were retained,
and in 1798, with the addition of six troops, they were formed
into the Regiment of Light Dragoons. The artillery of the Legion became the Corps of Artillerists and Engineers, later with
the designation of regiment. Still later, the Engineers became a
separate branch and, while the Regiment of Artillerists was
continued, a Regiment of Light Artillery was formed in 1808.
The riflemen of the Legion formed a battalion in 1799 and a
regiment in 1808.

The fortunes of the United States Army varied according to the anxiety of the United States Congress and its reactions to the threat of war. Twelve Regiments of Infantry were authorized by Congress in 1798, when war with France seemed likely. Colonels and majors were commissioned for the new regiments, but troops were not enlisted and in 1800 Congress discharged all twelve of the new regiments. Two years later, the 3rd and 4th Regiments of Infantry were erased from the establishment.

In 1808 Congress again became defense-minded, and it reactivated the 3rd, 4th, 5th, 6th, and 7th Regiments of Infantry, and increased the strength of the Regiment of Light Dragoons. With the approach of the War of 1812, eighteen new infantry, two new artillery, and one more Light Dragoon Regiment were authorized and implemented by Congress. Before that war was over in 1815, Congress had authorized Infantry Regiments through the 48th, as well as 17 companies of Rangers, part of whom, however, were considered as one of the Infantry Regiments authorized by the Act of 29 January 1813. The end of the War of 1812 saw the standing army of the United States reduced by consolidating all the Infantry Regiments into eight regiments. The Corps of Artillery absorbed some of the Infantry Regiments and the Light Dragoons, and it had a peacetime establishment of eight battalions. No mounted troops remained in service.

The regular army, which had been so reluctantly created for the western frontier, remained on that frontier. Even during the War of 1812 the army remained either in the West or on the New York frontier with Upper and Lower Canada. When Washington City was threatened in August 1814, only 125

Light Dragoons and 400 men from 3 Infantry Regiments could be found to make a defense of the capital of the nation. Even after the capital was burned, Congress remained suspicious of a standing army. The army was kept far away, on the limits of the nation, fighting the red man in the west and south. Only in the forts built to guard the harbors along the east coast did citizens see soldiers of the artillery sitting out years of boring duty behind stone walls. Up the Hudson a small group of young men studied to be soldiers at the United States Military Academy, founded in 1802. They were rarely seen or noticed, for when their studies were done most of them went west or south, where the scattered regiments of the regular army were pushing the frontiers toward oceans far from a Congress deliberating in Washington City.

Chronology of Actions and Events in the Northwest

1787	Northwest Territory established (Ohio, Indiana, Illinois, Michigan, Wisconsin, eastern Minnesota).
19–22 Oct. 1790	Colonel Harmar's defeat.
4 Nov. 1791	General St. Clair's defeat.
1 June 1792	Kentucky admitted to statehood.
20 Aug. 1794	General Wayne's victory at Fallen Timbers.
3 Aug. 1795	Treaty of Greenville.
4 July 1800	Indiana established as a Territory.
1 Mar. 1803	Ohio admitted to statehood.
30 June 1805	Michigan established as a Territory.
12 Aug. 1810	Governor Harrison confronts Tecumseh at Vincennes, Indiana.
7 Nov. 1811	General Harrison's victory at Tippecanoe Creek.
18 June 1812	U. S. declares war on Great Britain.
12 July 1812	General Hull invades Upper Canada.

17 July 1812   Mackinac Island surrenders to the British.

15 Aug. 1812   Fort Dearborn abandoned, garrison ambushed.

16 Aug. 1812   General Hull surrenders Detroit to General Brock.

5 Sept. 1812   Fort Madison attacked by Indians.

3–16 Sept. 1812 Fort Harrison attacked by Indians.

5–10 Sept. 1812 Fort Wayne attacked by Indians.

8 Oct. 1812   Lt. Elliott, U.S.N., captures *Caledonia* and *Detroit.*

13 Oct. 1812   General Brock killed at Queenston Heights.

18–22 Jan. 1813 General Winchester defeated at River Raisin; massacre at Frenchtown follows.

Mar.–July 1813   Indian raids and counter-raids in Indiana and Illinois.

28 Apr.–
9 May 1813   General Harrison defends Fort Meigs.

5 May 1813   Colonel Dudley defeated near Fort Meigs.

26 July 1813   Tecumseh menaces Fort Meigs.

2 Aug. 1813   General Procter attacks Fort Stephenson.

10 Sept. 1813   Commodore Perry's victory on Lake Erie.

27 Sept. 1813   General Harrison invades Upper Canada.

5 Oct. 1813   General Harrison's victory at the River Thames; Tecumseh killed in the battle.

Place Names and Modern Locations

Big Bottom	Near Marietta, Ohio
Black Rock	Buffalo, New York
Fort Campus Martius	Marietta, Ohio
Cleveland	Cleveland, Ohio
Fort Dearborn	Chicago, Illinois
Fort Defiance	Defiance, Ohio
Fort Deposit	Near Waterville, Ohio
Dunlap Station	Near Cincinnati, Ohio
Fort Erie (British)	Fort Erie, Ontario
Fort Findlay	Findlay, Ohio
Fort Franklin	Franklin, Ohio
Frenchtown	Monroe, Michigan
Fort George (British)	Mackinac Island, Michigan
Fort George (British)	Niagara on the Lake, Ontario
Fort Hamilton	Hamilton, Ohio
Fort Harmar	Near Marietta, Ohio
Fort Harrison	Terre Haute, Indiana
Fort Jefferson	Fort Jefferson, Ohio
Kickapoo Town	North end of Peoria Lake, Illinois
Fort Knox	Vincennes, Indiana

Legionville	Beaver, Pennsylvania
Lower Sandusky	Fremont, Ohio
Fort McArthur	Near Kenton, Ohio
Mackinac	Mackinac Island, Michigan
Fort Madison	Near Bellview, Illinois
Fort Malden (British)	Amherstburg, Ontario
Fort Meigs	Near Maumee, Ohio
Fort Miami (British)	Near Maumee, Ohio
Pigeon Roost Settlement	Southwest Indiana
Piqua (old)	Dayton, Ohio
Piqua (new)	Piqua, Ohio
Prophets Town	Near Battle Ground, Indiana
Fort Recovery	Fort Recovery, Ohio
St. Joseph's Island	Lake Huron, Ontario
Seneca Town	Seneca, Ohio
Fort Stephenson	Fremont, Ohio
Upper Sandusky	Upper Sandusky, Ohio
Fort Washington	Cincinnati, Ohio
Washington City	Washington, D.C.
Fort Wayne	Fort Wayne, Indiana
Fort William (British)	Thunder Bay, Ontario
Fort Winchester	Defiance, Ohio

Notes on Sources

"Listen to the tales of the old men" is an axiom for young historians. Benson J. Lossing did more than this. He sought out the old men, and wrote the tales they told him in *The Pictorial Field-Book of the War of 1812*. Lossing's sub-title is even more descriptive: "Illustrations, by Pen and Pencil, of the History, Biography, Scenery, Relics, and Traditions of the Last War for American Independence." Of particular value to the writer today are Lossing's pictures and description of the scenes of places that have since been obliterated by modern construction. Benson Lossing must be considered a primary source, but he must be used with discrimination by an author working today.

The same discrimination must be applied to the contemporary journals, particularly when they tell of events in which the journalist was not directly involved. Many of the journals of soldiers in the long war for the old American Northwest are preserved and can readily be found in the printed collections and publications of state and private historical societies. The author notes with regret and curiosity that the journals of the Northwest War (1790–1813) are by no means as vivid or as numerous as the personal accounts of the American War of Independence. Perhaps more people in the East were literate. Certainly the New Englanders were inveterate diary-keepers, but only before they moved into the West.

In the part of this book dealing with the biographies of the U.S. Army, and its officers and its regiments, Francis B. Heitman's *Historical Register of the United States Army* was invaluable. In *Canada's Soldiers,* George Stanley sorts out and explains the defense organization in Canada. The "Military Uniforms in America" series of prints, put out by the Company of Military Historians, shows graphically what the soldiers, American and British, regulars and militia, looked like on parade and on campaign.

In general, writers of the present time have ignored the complexities of the War of 1812 as a whole. Francis F. Beirne's *The War of 1812* is an exception, with excellent and detailed accounts of wars within that war. C. S. Forester's *The Age of Fighting Sail* tells the story of the naval war and contains an exciting account of Perry's battle on Lake Erie. *The War of 1812 in the Old Northwest,* by Alec R. Gilpin, is a painstaking and detailed study and interpretation, and contains a comprehensive bibliography of the transmontane war.

Index